When it comes to planting new churches, few know this territory better than Phil Stevenson. His vision is huge, his thinking is clear, and his experience is strong. His book, *Becoming a Ripple Church: Why and How to Plant New Congregations* offers proven and practical strategies for multiplying churches. Let's be candid—we desperately need to launch more new and vibrant churches. This book will help us all make that a reality.

—DAN REILAND, executive pastor, 12Stone Church;
author of *Amplified Leadership*

Becoming a Ripple Church challenges today's emerging leaders to embrace their role as catalysts for church multiplication. This resource is filled with practical, biblical methods that when implemented make "churches planting churches" the new normal.

—GARY REINECKE, ministry coach and trainer, InFocus

Phil Stevenson's concepts and research are tried and true. His heart for new churches is legendary. I hope that thousands of young leaders will pick up this book and start new churches. I pray that many older pastors will pick up this book and help start new churches. This book gives you the nuts and bolts that you need in order to spread the gospel effectively through new churches.

—GIL STIEGLITZ, executive pastor, Adventure Christian Church,
Roseville, California; author of *Leading a Thriving Ministry*

Every person has the opportunity to make an impact—positive or negative—every day. The same is true for churches. As Phil Stevenson points out in his book, *Becoming a Ripple Church*, it takes intentionality to "go and make" a difference for the kingdom of Jesus Christ. In this ready-made plan for making an eternal splash for Christ, you'll not only learn about a doable model for parenting churches, you'll understand what the Holy Spirit wants to accomplish through your life and church that will transform lives, churches, and communities with the hope and holiness of Jesus Christ.

—Jim Dunn, executive director, Church Multiplication
and Discipleship, The Wesleyan Church

Church planting is the single most effective form of evangelism, and Phil Stevenson knows how to do it better than anyone I've ever met. *Becoming a Ripple Church* is an excellent and practical guide for launching new congregations. We have a thriving daughter church as a direct result of following the outstanding suggestions offered in this book.

—Mark O. Wilson, senior pastor, Hayward Wesleyan Church;
author of *Filled Up, Poured Out*

BECOMING A RIPPLE CHURCH

BECOMING A RIPPLE CHURCH

WHY AND HOW TO PLANT NEW CONGREGATIONS

PHIL STEVENSON

wesleyan
publishing
house

Indianapolis, Indiana

Copyright © 2004, 2013 by Wesleyan Publishing House
Published by Wesleyan Publishing House
Indianapolis, Indiana 46250
Printed in the United States of America
ISBN: 978-0-89827-746-3
ISBN (e-book): 978-0-89827-747-0

The Library of Congress has catalogued a previous edition as follows:

Stevenson, Phil.
    The ripple church / Phil Stevenson.
        p. cm.—(The leading pastor series)
    Includes bibliographical references.
    ISBN 0-89827-271-8 (pbk.)
    1. Church development, New. I. Title. II. Series.
    BV652.24.S74 2004
    254'.1—dc22
                                        2003027553

This book was previously released as *The Ripple Church*.

This book is dedicated to the men and women who have courageously committed themselves to leading their churches in becoming multiplying congregations. It is the vision that they have beyond their local setting that has wide impact and influence for the gospel.

CONTENTS

FOREWORD
CHURCH PLANTING: DON'T FEAR

I love church planting because I love seeing people reached for the gospel.

But over the last twenty-five years I've been involved, church planting has changed—locally and globally. And how churches, networks, and denominations deal with church planting has changed as well. Today, more people are asking how we (who make up those churches, networks, and denominations) should consider and engage in church planting.

With that in mind, I'd offer some advice based on what I've seen. It's quite simple advice for churches and denominations: Simply don't be afraid.

Over the last few decades, I have observed that the main hindrance for churches, denominations, and leaders engaging in church planting is fear.

The very nature of church planting usually puts planters on the forefront of innovation within their generation. One of the reasons they are so effective at reaching the unchurched and dechurched is because they often allow the "how" of church planting to be shaped by the "who, when, and where" of culture. Giving space for this to happen can be a scary thing for other church and denominational leaders. Churches, denominations, and leaders are afraid that church plants are too innovative, take too much sacrifice, and are too difficult with which to cooperate.

Those fears must be overcome for church planting efforts to thrive in the future.

OVERCOME FEAR

If we want to see a church multiplication movement like Warren Bird and I talk about in *Viral Churches*, we need to choose to overcome fear.

This fear—of the new generation and their church planting activity—remains in many denominations, though thankfully, not all. We must get rid of the fear that keeps us "doing church" the same way and for only one group of people. As long as a church meets the biblical definition of a church and has the biblical marks of a church, it can look and function many different ways.

What should drive us is a confessional identity that we believe together a certain set of tenets (which will be different for different denominations) and being committed to confessional identity with missional cooperation. The result will be all kinds of church plants with one common confession and mission. And that is worth the effort.

BE WILLING TO SACRIFICE

Church plants take sacrifice, and that scares some people. Church plants also require new ways to cooperate, and that scares some people.

If churches and denominations won't sacrifice, they won't reproduce. It will involve the sacrifices of sending people to start a new church, creating some controversy in the denomination, and funding that could go to other needs (with vocal constituencies). If churches and denominations won't sacrifice, they won't reproduce.

BUILD COOPERATION

Finally, if a true multiplication movement is to take place, it will require reconsidering the ways in which we cooperate. Instead of demanding methodological conformity, we should celebrate sharing common beliefs with a common confession and missional cooperation in different settings. In the process, we can open up new lanes for new church planters and see a revolutionary church multiplication movement in this country once again.

Yes, church planting can be scary. But Phil Stevenson is an experienced guide. In *Becoming a Ripple Church*, Stevenson inspires readers to become actively involved in church parenting and provides clear practical steps for planting a church from an existing congregation.

Written from experience, *Becoming a Ripple Church* effectively motivates planting new churches with biblical wisdom. It is full of real-life stories and experiences, as well as practical insights that will help readers overcome their fears of church planting.

If churches, denominations, and leaders can overcome these fears, I believe we can—and will—see a church multiplication movement that will be both faithful and fruitful in our missional mandate to spread the gospel.

—ED STETZER
president of LifeWay Research, author, speaker, pastor, church planter, and Christian missiologist

ACKNOWLEDGEMENTS

To my wife, Joni, who has been a constant encouragement in my sharing of the ripple church vision.

To the Wesleyan Publishing House editing team led by Kevin Scott.

To my grandchildren, and to their peers, who will benefit from new churches communicating the gospel in a manner that will connect with them.

INTRODUCTION
THE RIPPLE CHURCH

You've seen the image a thousand times. A rock is tossed into a pond. The rock makes a splash. Ripples emanate from the point of impact, spreading across the surface of the water until they reach the other shore. We call it the ripple effect.

In that same way, a new generation of churches is creating a ripple effect across the country. Led by men and women of vision, these congregations are extending their influence out from the center, into their communities and across their regions.

How?

A few courageous leaders have done what few in the twenty-first-century church are willing to do. They have turned their focus outward, planting new churches rather than simply gathering more people into existing ones. These ripple churches have become points of impact, generating a movement that is spreading around the world.

But it hasn't been easy for them. By choosing influence (evangelism and outreach) over influx (church growth), ripple churches have sacrificed their own comfort and security in order to bring forth the next generation of Christians. They have abandoned contemporary notions of success in order to bring about kingdom growth. They have been willing to swim against the stream of popular culture.

Is it worth it?

Nimbus Dam is located roughly fifteen miles east of downtown Sacramento, California, a short jaunt along the Highway 50 corridor toward the south shore of Lake Tahoe. Nimbus Dam controls the water flow of the American River as it makes its way west toward the Sacramento River and, ultimately, to the Pacific Ocean.

The river's current can be brisk, especially in the fall, when an extraordinary event occurs each year. Every autumn thousands of salmon make their way east from the ocean, swimming against the river's west-flowing current. The fish head upriver in order to spawn. The journey requires tremendous energy, and many salmon die along the way. But they make this trip, swimming against the flow, in order to reproduce. If they don't, their species will not survive.

The salmon could, I suppose, live out their lives downstream. It would be more comfortable for them, with no current to fight and no risk to them. Upstream territory is unknown to them. To swim upstream demands an effort they may not be able to muster. Yet these creatures seem to know that something exists upstream that can be found nowhere else: the opportunity to create a new generation.

In fact, the salmon that make their way against the current each fall are themselves the product of a preceding generation's effort. Their predecessors expended the energy to swim against the tide so that they too could create new life. Every year yet another generation of salmon will make that same journey. The cycle of growth continues.

Today, the church desperately needs a new generation of leaders that is willing to swim against the current of contemporary church experience. Too many of us enjoy the relative calm of downstream life. We convince ourselves that gathering more people around us in a single church will ensure the existence of the Christian species. It won't. A large school of salmon swimming comfortably in their familiar ocean atmosphere will not survive indefinitely. Those salmon must fight their way upstream to create new life. Similarly, we must sacrifice our time, energy, and money if we are to create new congregations. The survival of the church depends upon it.

Planting churches will never be easy. In our current church culture, bigger is considered better. We measure ourselves by buildings, bodies, and budgets, and our bottom line is weekly worship attendance. In such a climate, the idea of planting new churches out of existing ones can raise a few eyebrows. Therefore, leaders who participate in the church-planting movement must swim against popular opinion. They must be willing to abandon commonly held notions about achievement and success.

To stay downstream is much easier. Yet, as Zig Ziglar noted, even a dead fish can swim downstream. The kind of multiplication that will ensure the future of the church can never happen in the downstream culture. We need to swim against the current.

So the challenge for today's church leaders is twofold: First, we must realize the need to propagate the gospel by multiplying congregations; and second, we must make sacrifices in order to do so. That will mean resisting the temptation merely to grow larger as a congregation, and that will require faith.

We risk much by swimming upstream. It's always easier to stay where we are, complacent and comfortable. We need leaders who have the God-given faith to move forward in spite of fear and uncertainty. By stepping out in faith, we will lay the foundation for an entire new generation of believers. Lives will be transformed. The church will be revolutionized. The entire world will be changed.

Will you accept this challenge? Will you move beyond the small circle of your own comfort and begin the ripple that will affect your community and your world? I saw a television advertisement that touted its product this way: "It began with a drop that caused a ripple, which caused a wave, which caused the whole world to stand up and take notice." One drop does make a difference. One leader can begin a great movement. One ripple can change the world.

Will it begin with you?

PART 1
WHY PARENT CHURCHES?

THE DIMMING OF THE CHURCH

In a recent conversation that I had with Ed Stetzer—author, missiologist, lecturer, church planter, and president of LifeWay Research—he told me, "The church in North America no longer has home-field advantage." He was saying that the church is no longer a key element of North American culture. We cannot assume that people in our society have a basic understanding of the church or of Christianity. The once-bright light of the church is quickly dimming.

We need to heed the voices of concern.

North America has transitioned from being at the center of Christianity to becoming a largely unchurched culture, says Joel Comiskey, cell church expert: "North America has so many unchurched people that it's now one of the mission targets of Christians who live in other countries."[1] This transitional reality seems to go largely unnoticed or ignored by church leaders today. Many point to the megachurch as an example of continued effectiveness in reaching North American culture. However, Comiskey paints another picture: "Often we define church growth by whether a few congregations are growing, rather than looking at the overall church in the nations. It's easy to point to certain megachurches and imagine that North America is exploding with church growth. Statistics, however, point to another reality."[2] The fact that a few churches are growing is misleading and tends to instill an unwarranted optimism.

Comiskey, who is a church planter, has discovered the statistical reality that "18 [percent] of US churches are growing primarily by transfer growth [and] 1 [percent] of the churches are growing by conversion growth."[3] This objective measure ought to give the North American church pause as it strategizes to effectively reach a culture that continues to distance itself from the gospel. Mike Regele of the Percept Group observes the challenge of the widening chasm between church culture and the changing shape of society: "Throughout most of the twentieth century the larger culture began to noticeably separate from the traditional churched culture—and it did so with ever increasing speed as the century drew to a close. As we move forward into the twenty-first century, the churched culture and changing shape of American society continue to grow further apart. It is this growing gap that contributes to the reality that mission in the twenty-first-century North America is cross-cultural."[4] The Great Commission, Jesus' evangelism mandate to his followers, is not to go and bring others from another church but to "go and make disciples of all the nations" (Matt. 28:19). "All the nations" includes North America.

While Christians rejoice that some individual churches are growing larger, this growth alone will not meet the challenges of the twenty-first century. Gaining new church members alone will not effectively engage the changing landscape of North American culture. We need to start new churches. New churches are better leveraged to connect with those who do not seek their spirituality from the existing church. Regele states, "Church planting is necessary for the church to stay relevant in the twenty-first century."[5]

The church must not be content with growth, but must pursue expansion. The Holy Spirit must be trusted to move the church beyond property lines and outside defined brick-and-mortar walls so it can break through preconceived barriers of evangelistic effectiveness.

The growth of the church and its ability to effectively engage the culture in which it finds itself will require a combination of two things: current Christ-followers sharing the gospel, and existing churches being willing to start new ones. This is not an either/or proposition but a both/and necessity. Pastor and church founder Fred Herron, in his book *Expanding God's Kingdom through Church Planting*, emphasizes this connection: "Both church planting and church renewal are needed but a focus on church planting prevails."[6]

Lyle Schaller, church growth consultant, observes, "Historically, new congregations have turned out to be the most effective approach to reaching new generations of people."[7] Underscoring Schaller's comment, Elmer Towns, cofounder of Liberty University and dean for its School of Religion, in his foreword written for *Spin-Off Churches*, states, "Church planting is not a denominational priority; any church can plant a new one. Church planting is not the outgrowth of a particular theology. All groups can do it whether Presbyterian, Baptist, Pentecostal, Mennonite, Community, or other. Church planting is not a strategy of megachurches; all churches can plant a new one."[8] Church planting is a methodology for kingdom expansion that crosses denominational lines.

Christianity no longer holds priority in our culture today. Many existing churches are unable to transition enough to meet the demands of this new mind-set. However, existing churches can help spawn new congregations to address this changing climate.

I have been a fan of college football coach Lou Holtz for years. Holtz has had an amazing career. He led Notre Dame to a national championship in 1988; he has coached four different college teams to top-twenty national rankings; and he has won 238 regular season games and twelve bowl games. In 2001 Holtz engineered the turnaround of the University of South Carolina football program, leading a team that had been winless just two years before to a post-season bowl victory. In forty-three years of coaching, Lou Holtz has consistently demonstrated the ability to produce champions.

What's his secret?

In his book *Winning Every Day*, Holtz reveals one key for success. When making choices, he suggests, remember the letters WIN, which stand for the phrase "What's important now?"[1] Asking that simple question can help us to determine our priorities. It will ensure that we concentrate on first things first. Take it from me—it works!

I believe churches need to ask that question: What's important now? There are so many things we could be doing, but what *should* we be doing? What is our first priority? What is most important for the church of Jesus Christ right now?

The answer today is the same as it was when Jesus walked the earth. Just before he ascended into heaven, Jesus gave the church its marching orders. He identified the WIN priority for us when he said plainly, "Go and make disciples" (Matt. 28:19). The church is still in the disciple-making business. That has not changed, and until Christ returns, it never will. It's time to stop wringing our hands, wondering what we should be doing. We need to halt the endless meetings in which we discuss our purpose. Our mission is clear: Go make disciples! The most effective way of doing that, and the way we see modeled in the New Testament, is to create new congregations. That can be done by church planting, which means establishing an entirely new congregation, or by church parenting, which is creating a new church out of an existing one.

To evaluate the vitality of a business, consultants often ask its owners two questions: "What is your business?" and "How is business?" The answers always reveal the state of the company's health. Two similar questions will help us zero in on the condition of the church: "Are we going?" and "Are we making disciples?"

First, are we going? Is there a sending environment in the church today? What are we doing to create a sending atmosphere? Are we mobilizing people to infiltrate their culture, or do we have a come-to-us attitude? To go means to take Christ into our communities. It requires that we identify our spheres of influence and then spread the gospel within them. Every believer influences some people; that's given. What is less certain is our willingness to use that influence to imbue others with the presence of Jesus.

Second, are we making disciples? What are we doing to produce believers in Jesus Christ and to cultivate faith within them? Our mission is not only to win people to Christ, but also to wean them from the world. Disciple making is a long, arduous task. It involves meeting people where they are spiritually and moving them to where they need to be. It is relational, sometimes messy, but always meaningful.

Sadly, many churches would rather trade the difficult task of dealing with people for the easier task of developing programs. We prefer the quick-fix approach to making disciples that programs seem to offer. A new idea, a creative method, or a nicely packaged worship service may offer a short-term solution, but it will never fill the deep void in people's lives. Only a relationship with Christ can do that.

Several years ago I had a severe gall bladder attack and needed to have my gall bladder removed. During my hospital stay, a nurse offered me the painkiller Demerol. She asked, "Would you like it as a shot in your hip or through your IV?"

"What's the difference?" I asked.

She explained that injecting the drug through the IV would provide instant relief, while the hip shot would take several minutes to kick in. At the time my body needed instant relief. "Give me the IV," I said, and the nurse shot the painkiller into the intravenous tube. The drug entered my bloodstream immediately, and the result was awesome. A warm feeling began at the bottom of my feet and rushed through my body. My pain was alleviated, and I was happy. For the next day or so, I looked forward to the nurse's visit every four hours. Those IV injections brought immediate relief.

But they didn't bring healing. What my body really needed was to mend, to be made whole again. It would have been shortsighted and unhealthy if I had depended only on the shots. The injections made me feel better, but they didn't make me well.

In the same way, it is shortsighted and unhealthy to rely only on programs to treat the needs of the church. We need to make and to mature disciples of Christ; and to do that, we must go beyond where we are now. We need to accomplish more than what we can do in one place at one time. We must go out to engage our culture with the gospel.

Ripple churches understand the "Go and make" mission. They have made the choice to go beyond themselves, to reach the lost by planting or parenting multiplying churches. Ripple churches release people to go—and going is necessary for making disciples. That has been God's plan from the beginning.

GOD VALUES MULTIPLICATION 3

Multiplication has been a critical component of God's plan for humanity from the beginning. He firmly established this principle at the creation of the world: "Then God said, 'Let the land sprout with vegetation—every sort of seed-bearing plant, and trees that grow seed-bearing fruit. These seeds will then produce the kinds of plants and trees from which they came.' And that is what happened. The land produced vegetation—all sorts of seed-bearing plants, and trees with seed-bearing fruit. Their seeds produced plants and trees of the same kind. And God saw that it was good" (Gen. 1:11–12). God clearly established that he was not merely creating one thing, but instead creating a process of multiplication.

He created *seed-bearing* fruit and trees. It was the seed that enabled the creation to continue to produce, multiply, and flourish. It was the seed that provided the vegetation the opportunity to move beyond one generation. It is through the bearing of fruit that the creation participates with the Creator in the creative process. The creation and the Creator partner together. The creation is dependent on the Creator for its life. The Creator graciously allows the creation to be the conduit of his presence and reality to the world around us.

The multiplying character of God continued to flow in the creative process with his creation of fish and birds: "Then God said, 'Let the earth produce every sort of animal, each producing offspring of the same kind—livestock, small animals that scurry along the ground, and wild animals.' And that is what happened. God made all sorts of wild animals, livestock, and small animals, each able to produce offspring of the same kind. And God saw that it was good" (1:24–25). In the reproductive process, God finds joy, and he sees goodness in what is created.

God continued to initiate his multiplication principle in his creation of humanity: "So God created human beings in his own image. In the image of God he created them; male and female he created them. Then God blessed them and said, 'Be fruitful and multiply. Fill the earth'" (1:27–28). In creating humanity, God instructed the man and woman to multiply. This multiplication must be proficient; in other words, the earth was to be filled. Bruce Finn, church-planting coordinator, wrote in his dissertation for Reformed Theological Seminary, "While international missions and church planting are ordinarily thought of as concerns of the New Testament, their roots can be found deeply embedded in the soil of Old Testament history and theology. God's desire since the creation of mankind has been to fill the world with his people."[1] It was this multiplying creation that God called excellent: "Then God looked over all he had made, and he saw that it was very good!" (1:31).

This blessing of multiplication was renewed after the flood. Even man's sinfulness could not negate God's desire to have his creation multiply: "Release all the animals—the birds, the livestock, and the small animals that scurry along the ground—so they can be fruitful and multiply throughout the earth. . . . Then God blessed Noah and his sons and told them, 'Be fruitful and multiply. Fill the earth.' . . . Now be fruitful and multiply, and repopulate the earth (Gen. 8:17; 9:1, 7).

This sign of blessing was communicated to the patriarchs—to Abraham, Isaac, and Jacob. God said to Abraham, "I will certainly bless you. I will multiply your descendants beyond number, like the stars in the sky and the sand on the seashore" (22:17). He reaffirmed this blessing to Isaac: "Do not be afraid, for I am with you and will bless you. I will multiply your descendants" (26:24). God extended this promise of multiplication blessing to Jacob as well: "May God Almighty bless you and give you many children" (28:3).

Finn connects the work of God through Abraham and his descendants to his salvation plan for all mankind: "Abraham and his children would be the instruments of God through which He would implement His plan of salvation for fallen mankind. Though Abraham and his physical descendants would have a very significant role in the unfolding of God's redemptive purpose, the blessing they received from the Lord would have international implications."[2] Each of the patriarchs—Abraham, Isaac, and Jacob—was included in God's ongoing blessing of multiplication. The good news of God's redemption is replicable and sustainable if those charged with it are willing to move beyond generational and geographical limitations.

The blessing that God bestowed upon Abraham's descendants was not only for them. It was the beginning of God multiplying this blessing throughout all humankind. The blessing of multiplication, however, came with imperatives. It was not to be just for Abraham, but for those who followed after him. Church-planting expert Fred Herron suggests, "God was not choosing Abram [Abraham] and Israel through him, in an effort to exclude the other nations, but instead, he was choosing Israel to be a servant to other nations. From the beginning, Israel was to serve as an ambassador of God's redemptive purposes for all nations."[3] God's blessing was, through Israel, for the myriad of nations throughout history.

God's redemptive purpose was not to be confined to one person, people group, or culture. God's redemption is to be reproduced, or multiplied, in the lives of others. God's redemption must slowly, yet convincingly, saturate the entirety of the world. When those enfolded into the kingdom resist the multiplication of that kingdom, they oppose the God of eternity.

Jonah resisted this multiplication of faith. He enjoyed the kindness of God, yet he resisted the expanding of that kindness to those he deemed unworthy. God called him to "get up and go to the great city of Nineveh" (Jon. 1:2). But Jonah decided that such a mission was not for him. He chose to go in the "opposite direction to get away from the LORD" (1:3).

This resistance from Jonah spawned a series of events. These events would demonstrate God's desire to multiply his message of judgment, repentance, forgiveness, and hope.

Jonah ended up in the belly of a large fish. He repented of his ingrown attitudes and his selfish attitude regarding God's salvation and cried out to God. God heard Jonah's cry and reinstituted his call to the prophet. This reinstituted call models the graciousness of God to his people: "Then the LORD spoke to Jonah a second time: 'Get up and go to the great city of Nineveh, and deliver the message I have given you'" (3:1–2).

This time Jonah obeyed. He went to Nineveh and conveyed God's message. And "the people of Nineveh believed God's message" (3:5). It was through the people's belief that redemption entered into the Ninevite culture. The message ingrained itself into the fiber of the Ninevites' society. The people exhibited repentance. They responded in a tangible way. "When God saw what they had done and how they had put a stop to their evil ways, he changed his mind and did not carry out the destruction he had threatened" (3:10). The message of grace, forgiveness, and redemption had been reproduced in another nation. This had been God's intention back when he had called Abraham to be a blessing.

We often resist God's call to propagate, or multiply, the gospel message. Jonah, instead of rejoicing at the Ninevites' acts of remorse and repentance, reacted in frustration and anger: "This change of plans greatly upset Jonah, and he became very angry. So he complained to the LORD about it: 'Didn't I say before I left home that you would do this, LORD? That is why I ran away to Tarshish! I knew that you are a merciful and compassionate God, slow to get angry and filled with unfailing love. You are eager to turn back from destroying people" (4:1–2). Jonah was upset that the judgment he had spoken over Nineveh was not going to take place. This provides a glimpse into the selfishness that too often characterizes some of God's people. This same selfishness continues to manifest itself in the church today.

God's heart is for multiplication, but his people often rebel against his heart. We are content with individual salvation stories, and we resist helping others write their own stories. When this attitude finds its way into communities of faith, it produces ingrown and selfish churches that resist reaching out to those outside their own faith communities. They choose instead to possess the gift God has given them out of his gracious kindness. They cling to it. It belongs to them.

It was this kind of selfish possessiveness that caused the nation of Israel to turn inward. It was this selfish, possessive nature that led to Jonah's resistance to taking the message to Nineveh. It is this same ingrown nature that causes the Christ-followers of today to neglect the multiplication of our faith through its people and churches. Fred Herron makes clear the need for God's people to extend his kingdom to others: "God has always desired to establish a people under his rule in order to reveal himself more fully and to extend his rule through his people to all the nations on earth."[4]

God's original call for his people to multiply is extended to today's disciples. The time continuum from when God said "Let there be . . . and there was" to the present has not eroded his heart for the world. God still wants to use his followers to multiply his kingdom across generations, nations, and peoples.

If God's design was for the creation to multiply in like kind, why would the church not multiply itself? Disciples should multiply disciples, and churches should multiply churches. The world will never be infiltrated with the gospel unless the church is multiplied into every geographical and demographical area. This is best done through the planting of multiplying churches.

The heart of God for his people to multiply and expand his kingdom is evident from the beginning—from creation. God began the process of fruitful proliferation, and he expects his creation to carry it on. This truth finds its expression in the incarnational message of Jesus and in the ministry of those who follow him. Multiplication is God's plan. It should be the church's plan too.

4 THE NEW TESTAMENT IMPERATIVE

That which is healthy reproduces: "A good tree produces good fruit" (Matt. 7:17). A seed in fertile soil increases its productivity: "Still other seeds fell on fertile soil, and they produced a crop that was thirty, sixty, and even a hundred times as much as had been planted" (13:8). The combination of a willingness to plant seeds and right cultivation results in productivity.

God's people are to be productive. They are to multiply. And C. Peter Wagner, in *Church Planting for a Greater Harvest*, views church planting as the method for obeying God's command to extend the gospel: "Church planting is the New Testament way of extending the gospel. Trace the expansion of the church through Jerusalem, Judea, Samaria and the uttermost part of the earth and you will see that church planters led the way. This is the kingdom activity, strongly, endorsed by God our King. Collectively, as a community of the kingdom, we can scarcely feel that we are obeying God if we fail to plant churches and plant them intentionally and aggressively."[1] Multiplication expands the church's influence, exhibits fruit, and enlarges the kingdom.

Jesus mandated his followers to "go and make disciples of all the nations" (Matt. 28:19). This is a clear indication that growth and multiplication are expectations of God, not exceptions. Evangelization is not effectively done within the walls of the church. Christ followers need to *go*! This means going in our daily lives, but it also means moving out to establish new churches. Bill Sheeks, a leader in the Church of God (Cleveland), observes, "Church planting must be taken seriously because of its vast contribution to the kingdom of God."[2] Missiologist David Hesselgrave, in his work *Planting Churches Cross-Culturally*, states, "The primary mission of the church and, therefore, of the churches is to proclaim the Gospel of Christ and gather believers into local churches where they can be built up in the faith and made effective in service, thereby planting new congregations throughout the world."[3] Without a healthy faith community in which new believers can connect, there will be no disciples. And the mandate is for disciples.

Jesus desired his followers to be a proactive force in engaging the culture in which they resided. He did not seem compelled to gather his followers to himself to keep them, but rather to empower them to go. This sending mentality is woven throughout his earthly ministry. He embodied it. He taught it. He empowered his people for it.

It was through understanding his *sent* nature that Jesus fulfilled his own ministry. It was in this understanding that he found his purpose. He knew that God the Father had sent God the Son to humanity. And it is through this same knowledge of being sent by God that Christians find an avenue to spiritual vitality and sanctified wholeness:

- "For I have come down from heaven to do the will of God who sent me, not to do my own will" (John 6:38).
- "I live because of the living Father who sent me" (6:57).
- "Jesus told them, 'My message is not my own; it comes from God who sent me'" (7:16).
- "Jesus told them, 'If God were your Father, you would love me, because I have come to you from God. I am not here on my own, but he sent me'" (8:42).
- "Jesus shouted to the crowds, 'If you trust me, you are trusting not only me, but also God who sent me. For when you see me, you are seeing the one who sent me'" (12:44–45).

A genuine understanding of Jesus, his life, and his ministry is to be found in his *sent* nature.

God's saving act through Jesus is closely linked to his sending action. It was in the sending of Jesus that God expressed his redemptive nature unlike he ever had before. God had done acts of redemption prior to sending Jesus, but he had not been as personally present in those scenarios as he was in the person of Jesus. He had used prophets, kings, and others to share his story of deliverance. He had infused history with acts of power and awe-inspiring activity. But it was in sending Jesus that God immersed himself in creation. He plunged fully into the pool of humanity. He clothed himself in the garb of humanness. "Christ is the visible image of the invisible God" (Col. 1:15). It was in the sending of Jesus that God connected with those he loved.

When God immersed himself in the world in this way, through Jesus, he branded his stylistic approach.

Jesus challenged his followers to live out this *sentness*. Salvation is about more for us than simply being saved; we were saved in order to be sent. In the parables and in his interactions with those who chose to follow him, Jesus consistently pushed believers out toward others:

- "If a man has a hundred sheep and one of them wanders away, what will he do? Won't he leave the ninety-nine others on the hills and go out to search for the one that is lost?" (Matt. 18:12).
- "A farmer went out to plant some seed" (Mark 4:3).
- "Jesus himself sent them out from east to west with the sacred and unfailing message of salvation that he gives eternal life" (16:8).
- "One day Jesus called together his twelve disciples and gave them power and authority to cast out all demons and to heal all diseases. Then he sent them out to tell everyone about the Kingdom of God and to heal the sick" (Luke 9:1–2).
- "The harvest is great, but the workers are few. So pray to the Lord who is in charge of the harvest; ask him to send more workers into his fields. Now go, and remember that I am sending you out as lambs among wolves" (10:2–3).
- "You didn't choose me. I chose you. I appointed you to go and produce lasting fruit" (John 15:16).

The link between the Father who sent the Son and the Son who sends his followers is clear: "Just as you sent me into the world, I am sending them into the world" (17:18). God saved people not merely for themselves, but for the world that has yet to embrace him. God has a proactive nature. He initiated creation. He initiated the promise of blessing. He initiated the covenant. He initiated the plan of redemption. He initiated sending Jesus.

There is a natural inclination for Christ-followers to focus primarily on being with Jesus as opposed to representing him. A microcosm of this attitude is seen in Mark 5. In this passage, we read that Jesus freed a man of demon possession. The demons left the man and were allowed to enter some pigs, and the man was visibly and completely changed. This resulted in the community rising up against Jesus and asking him to leave their area (see Mark 5:17). Jesus honored their request. As he returned to his boat to depart, the freed demon-possessed man approached Jesus and "begged to go with him" (5:18).

In that moment, Jesus set into motion his plan for all those who follow him. The plan is for them to be used by God to infiltrate their societies and cultures for him. "Jesus said, 'No, go home to your family, and tell them everything the Lord has done for you and how merciful he has been'" (5:19).

Jesus was *sending* this new disciple back to his people. This newly freed man was to go into the harvest field and engage folks where they were. He would best be "with" Jesus as he went out for Jesus. This is living out the sent nature of God.

It is by believing in the one whom God *sent*—Jesus—that Christ followers embrace the mighty work of salvation: "This is the only work God wants from you: Believe in the one he has sent" (John 6:29). It is by believing in the one whom God sent that eternal life is gained: "And this is the way to have eternal life—to know you, the only true God, and Jesus Christ, the one you sent to earth" (17:3). It is by believing in the one whom God sent that his disciples go into the world: "I am in them and you are in me. May they experience such perfect unity that the world will know that you sent me and that you love them as much as you love me" (17:23).

God the Father sent God the Son. God the Son sent God the Spirit. In the power of God the Spirit, Christ's disciples are sent into the world as God's ambassadors. "But you will receive power when the Holy Spirit comes upon you. And you will be my witnesses, telling people about me everywhere—in Jerusalem, throughout Judea, in Samaria, and to the ends of the earth" (Acts 1:8).

The early church understood its role as a group of people who had been sent. They were to infiltrate their world, their societies, their cultures, and the people around them with the redemptive message of Christ.

The gospel was to extend to all peoples and cultures. This would only be achieved as God's people went and made more disciples. Elmer Towns of Liberty University highlights the implication of the Great Commission on church planting: "Most people recognize that the Great Commission commands Christians to evangelize unsaved people. Few people realize the implied method of carrying out this commission. The Great Commission implies that church planting is the primary method to evangelize the world. . . . God's primary method of evangelizing a new community is by planting a New Testament church to reach the area with the gospel."[4] The fulfillment of the Great Commission would be unlikely to happen apart from the multiplication of new churches.

Multiplication, evangelism, church planting, and churches planting churches together form a seamless movement of fulfilling the Great Commission, which is the primary task of God's people. We are to "go and make disciples" (Matt. 28:19). Church planting, primarily through existing churches daughtering other churches, is the best methodology to achieve God's plan. A church cannot abstain from planting churches and be a biblical church. God never intended that the church be just for us. His aim has always been to multiply the church, gathering more and more people to himself. Church planting is not for us; it is for God. Its goal is to gather more people to him. The biblical example is clear: The early church going out and making disciples is evident throughout the New Testament.

When we establish new congregations, we recapture the spirit of Acts—the spirit that compelled Christ-followers to start new communities of faith whenever and wherever people were drawn to the Lord. This is the Great Commission in action. Ed Stetzer, in his book *Planting Missional Churches*, shares how the early church used church planting to carry out the Great Commission imperative: "The earliest churches obeyed the Great Commission by planting new congregations to carry out the assignments of discipling, baptizing, and teaching that would begin the multiplication process of planting more and more churches."[5] Individual believers are to take seriously the command to go and make disciples. We are to be the incarnational presence of Christ to those around us.

Just as "Christ is the visible image of the invisible God" (Col. 1:15), so believers are the visible expression of Christ. Christ-followers are to multiply, creating more Christ-followers. This is disciple-making. However, the multiplication is not to simply stop with more and more disciples having been made. It needs to extend into building communities of faith.

Paul traveled the world making disciples. The new converts he won to Christ created the core of new faith communities. These faith communities were to represent Christ in their areas of responsibility (cities, towns, villages). These churches were to be salt and light where they were. They were to expand their influence through the starting of new congregations. Stetzer writes, "It's obvious by their actions that the first hearers of the Great Commission assumed its fulfillment required multiplying disciples and forming new congregations."[6]

The Antioch church was birthed when Christ-followers went out with the gospel message. Persecution had broken out against the church in Jerusalem, and as a result, many believers had fled the city: "A great wave of persecution began that day, sweeping over the church in Jerusalem; and all the believers except the apostles were scattered through the regions of Judea and Samaria" (Acts 8:1). When this happened, the believers practiced the most basic of evangelistic methodologies: where they were is where they shared.

The Antioch congregation then became a sending agency. It multiplied into other churches throughout the known world. The leaders at Antioch, with their visionary, evangelistic hearts, saw beyond their community into unreached areas: "Among the prophets and teachers of the church at Antioch of Syria were Barnabas, Simeon (called 'the black man'), Lucius (from Cyrene), Manaen (the childhood companion of King Herod Antipas), and Saul. One day as these men were worshiping the Lord and fasting, the Holy Spirit said, 'Dedicate Barnabas and Saul for the special work to which I have called them.' So after more fasting and prayer, the men laid their hands on them and sent them on their way" (Acts 13:1–3). The Antioch church had been the unintended result of persecution. But they determined to be more intentional in their expansion efforts than their founders had been.

Paul Becker and Mark Williams, in their handbook for daughter church planting, show how the sending nature of the Antioch church impacted the world: "In sending those two church planters [Paul and Barnabas], that church in Antioch became the mother church for all churches across what is today called Turkey and Greece. Later on churches across Europe and in modern times, North and South America, were also the result of the daughter church planting done by the church in Antioch."[7] The mission of the church is to relentlessly pursue the fulfillment of the Great Commission. The Antioch church modeled this. Its members called out and commissioned their best believers to carry on the heart of God through going and making.

The Great Commission expresses God's sending and multiplying nature. Christ made this mandate a priority for his people, and it is to be implemented by the faith communities that are established in his name.

God sent prophets and teachers. He sent his Son. He is now sending his church. And a critical component in carrying out the biblical imperative to fulfill the Great Commission is church planting, as the authors of *Spin-Off Churches* affirm: "Church planting is not only biblical; it is essential to fulfilling the Great Commission."[8]

REACHING A REGION 5

Many church leaders today want to develop regional churches, which gather people from a broad region to worship in a single place. These leaders expect to attract people from their surrounding communities to attend their own churches, and locals often respond to these leaders' overtures. People will drive some distance to the church's primary ministry facility.

The philosophy of these churches is that of ministry by influx. The leaders ask, "How many people can we gather together at one place at one time?" A regional ministry, however, as opposed to a regional church, is built on a different philosophy: ministry by influence. Leaders of regional ministries ask, "Whom are we influencing with the gospel?" Their goal is to create diverse ministries that can reach diverse peoples, and they plant various kinds of churches in order to achieve that goal.

Not every church can be a regional church, but every church can have a regional ministry, extending its influence over a broad area. By helping to multiply churches, every congregation can extend its influence throughout its region.

Applebee's Neighborhood Grill and Bar, a well-known restaurant chain, provides a business analogy to regional ministry. Consider its formula for growth, which it calls "conscious cannibalization." Most restaurant chains carefully space their stores so that the sales of one don't eat into the sales of another. But Applebee's floods a territory with stores in order to gain brand recognition and market dominance. When most chains were building bigger and bigger restaurants, Applebee's designed smaller units, which were cheaper and faster to build as well as easier to fill on slow days.[1]

It is possible for churches to adopt a similar regional mentality, which promotes the success of several locations in an area, not just one or two. The question for church leaders is whether they want a regional church or a regional ministry. As a church leader, are you interested in creating one successful church that gathers people from a broad region, or would you like to see many churches thriving throughout a given area?

OUT FROM THE CENTER

I have lived in California most of my life, and a great deal of those years were spent in Southern California. California is well-known for its Hollywood glitter, wonderful weather, trendsetting fashions, and eccentric celebrities. But nothing attracts the attention of nonnative Californians more than an earthquake.

Earthquakes vary in their intensity and duration. But they all have something in common—an epicenter. The epicenter of an earthquake is the location of the quake's origin; it is where all the activity begins. All the energy flows from the epicenter.

Just as each earthquake is different from others, reaching a region with the gospel may happen in various ways. But every type of ministry emanates from an epicenter—the local church. The church that chooses to have a regional reach will involve itself in church planting. Church-planting energy does not flow from denominational headquarters, departments of evangelism, seminaries, parachurch organizations, or any other source. It flows from the local church. Existing churches exude the energy, creativity, and impetus needed to infiltrate their regions and, ultimately, the world.

It's time for us to return to our biblical roots and spread the gospel by multiplying congregations. It is through the multiplying of new congregations that regions will be reached with the gospel message. Local churches must include this work of parenting new churches as an integral part of their regional evangelistic plan.

Spreading the gospel by parenting multiplying congregations is not a new idea—nor is it optional for a Bible-believing, evangelistic congregation. It is the approach modeled in Scripture, and there is simply no other way to meet the great needs of a desperate world.

6 EVANGELISTIC EFFECTIVENESS

In his book *Church Planting for a Greater Harvest*, C. Peter Wagner boldly declares, "The single most effective evangelistic methodology under heaven is planting new churches."[1] In my experience, such a statement always elicits a strong reaction. Whenever I share this idea with a group of pastors, I can count on immediate feedback. Some will ask, "Does that mean that if I don't participate in planting churches, I'm not doing effective evangelism?" Others retort, "I don't agree with that. We are reaching many people for Christ, and we don't plant churches."

Once people get over the shock of the assertion, however, I am able to point out that Dr. Wagner does not propose that church planting is the *only* viable evangelistic methodology, but that it is the *most effective* one. If Wagner is correct, then every evangelistic church should want to participate in this movement. Effective churches employ every means they can to reach the world for Christ. Church planting must be a part of a full-orbed approach to evangelism.

WHY IT WORKS

The Church Multiplication Training Center reports the following statistics on the average number of converts produced by churches each year per one hundred members:

- Churches zero- to three-years-old: 10
- Churches three- to fifteen-years-old: 5
- Churches over fifteen-years-old: 1.5[2]

Obviously, new churches do a better job of bringing people to Christ than more-established churches do. Lyle Schaller adds this insight: "Planting new churches is the closest we have to a guaranteed means of reaching more people with the Good News that Jesus Christ is Lord and Savior. The historical record is clear that we cannot rely on long-established congregations to reach all the new generations of people."[3]

Why are new churches so effectively reaching the lost, disenfranchised, and unchurched? There are several reasons.

ATTRACTION

When I was a kid, I spent many hot summer evenings out on the front porch, the coolest spot around our house. I remember seeing all kinds of moths and other insects milling around the porch light. They were attracted to its light and warmth. People are similarly attracted to the energy and vitality of a new venture.

A Mexican restaurant opened recently in our area, and my family and I decided to try it. We arrived for an early dinner at about 5:30 p.m., a time when there is typically no waiting line at our local restaurants. We were surprised to find that there was already a twenty-minute wait for a table. That restaurant was not the only one offering Mexican cuisine that evening, but it was the newest one doing so. Most patrons were there for the same reason we were: They wanted to try something new.

That's one reason a new church is more likely to catch the attention of those who are looking for a church experience. Some people feel the need to attend church, but they put it off, because they view the churches around them as too rigid or too difficult to break into. Parenting a new church provides a fresh opportunity for people to get plugged in. There are unchurched people who pass by your church every week, some of whom are looking for something new. You can offer it to them. Parenting a new church provides entry points for those who have found reasons to stay away from established congregations.

I once had the opportunity to preach at the opening service of a church in Southern California. After the service, I met a single mom who held in her hand one of the flyers that the church had sent out by mail. When I asked the woman why she had decided to come to church, she said, "I just moved to the area, and I wanted to get my kids into church. When this flyer came in the mail, I thought this might be a good time to start." New things attract new people.

CAMARADERIE

Bonds between people are more easily formed in a church that is just beginning. Everyone is new, so it's easier for people to form relationships with each other. People who have never attended church or who have not attended in quite some time know that in a place in which everything is new, they will not be alone in their need to make new friends. They won't have to break into existing relationships and group structures.

Something similar happens when people move into a new area. There is a huge difference between moving into an established neighborhood and moving into a new one. I have done both, and it is far easier to establish friendships with neighbors in a new development. Everyone who lives in the area is a newcomer, and that forms a common bond among them. The same is true in a new church. Everyone enters in together.

URGENCY

Another reason new churches are more effective at evangelism is that they have to be. Most existing churches can support themselves, at least for awhile, even when no new people are being reached. Established churches have a solid core and can meet their budget with the existing group. But that kind of self-sufficiency can result in complacency. Before long, an established church may make only token efforts to reach outsiders.

A new church, on the other hand, must grow in order to thrive. Its future depends on an influx of new people who are learning stewardship, deepening their faith, and developing their leadership abilities. Without a stream of new believers, the new church will die in its early stages.

FOCUS

New churches are on the cutting edge of the church's purpose—winning the disconnected, disenfranchised, and dissatisfied to

Christ. They are not preoccupied with maintenance, because they have nothing to maintain. They want to move out and gain new territory. Not content with holding the beachhead, they want to take the entire island.

A man walked into a Circle K store. He placed a twenty-dollar bill on the counter and asked for change. When the clerk opened the cash drawer, the man pulled a gun and demanded all the cash. The cashier complied with the gunman's demand, and rightly so. The robber then took the cash and fled. In his haste, however, the gunman left the original twenty-dollar bill on the counter. And how much did he get from the cash drawer? Fifteen dollars. It actually cost the man five dollars to rob the store![4]

Too many long-established churches leave the twenty on the counter. They lose sight of their original purpose and actually shrink, in kingdom terms, rather than grow. New churches, on the other hand, seldom lose sight of their purpose. They're focused on reaching the lost for Christ.

FLEXIBILITY

New churches are flexible; they make changes more readily than existing churches do. They do not live under the prohibitions of the past. In an established church, the familiar words, "We've never done that before," often become a roadblock to change. In a new church, "We've never done that before" is an invitation to try. New churches are like speedboats; established churches are like supertankers. Having a speedboat mentality allows new congregations to make adjustments or to change direction with little effort. New churches are usually willing to do whatever it takes to reach people for Christ.

Vintage Church is a four-year-old congregation located in Randleman, North Carolina. Originally, the church had been in Greensboro, about twenty miles from Randleman. But one of its core team members was a high school vice principal in Randleman. He began a youth ministry that grew at a steady pace, so the church had a youth group meeting in Randleman and Sunday morning worship in Greensboro. It soon became evident that the church would get more traction by leveraging the youth ministry in Randleman, so the members moved the Sunday worship and ministry target from Greensboro to Randleman.

Established churches have difficulty moving worship to a new time frame, much less to a whole new community. New churches are more flexible and willing to adjust. This makes them a key commodity in today's quickly changing societal environment.

SPECIFICITY

New churches are effective at evangelism because they can afford to target the specific needs of people groups. New congregations don't have a host of stakeholders, each with an agenda, and they don't have to expend energy maintaining existing programs. Instead, new churches are free to aim their ministry at anyone they choose. They can focus on doing a few things well rather than doing many things with mediocrity.

Planet Fitness was started in 1992. It branded itself as the anti-fitness club. Its founders wanted to create a judgment-free environment that would encourage those interested in fitness to get off the couch and into the gym. As a result, the club does not choose to target hardcore body builders. CEO and cofounder Michael Grondahl says, "We also provide weights, but our gyms don't include any of the big, heavy equipment that bodybuilders use. Bodybuilders don't really have any reason to join our gym, which is fine."[5] This is what new churches are able to do: be specific with no apologies.

MULTIPLICATION

Rabbits are known for being prolific breeders. Leave a male and female rabbit together for very long, and you'll soon have lots of little bunnies. Something similar happens with church plants—they tend to be prolific at reproducing themselves. When churches begin to parent reproducing churches, the number of churches in an area increases dramatically in a short time.

Is it impossible for established churches to incorporate these effectiveness factors into their evangelism strategies? Of course not. But by and large, established churches will never be as effective at evangelism as new churches. Senior adults can get into good physical condition and even run marathons, but an older person will never run as well as a younger one. Youth have energy. That's true for churches as well. All congregations, regardless of age, should be winning people to Christ. Yet we must recognize the evangelistic vitality of new congregations and do all we can to capitalize upon it. New churches reach more people for Christ. Therefore, planting churches is the single most effective method of evangelism.

WHAT TO DO ABOUT IT

Perhaps you have never entertained the idea of parenting a church. You may have determined that God has called you to build a single large church, not to parent new ones. Yet even so, you may sense a change in your spirit. Perhaps you recognize that increasing the size of one congregation and planting new churches are not mutually exclusive aims. You may realize that church planting is an effective evangelistic method and feel prompted to participate in that calling.

If you do, it is the beginning of a God-given dream.

One day Jesus planted a dream in the heart of Peter. Jesus was teaching by the Sea of Galilee, and the crowds had pushed him to the water's edge. Jesus asked Peter if he might sit in the fisherman's boat to teach, and Peter honored the request. But it was after Jesus finished teaching that Peter's real lesson began.

Jesus asked Peter to push out into deep water and let his nets down for a catch. Peter was not thrilled by this suggestion. He and his partners had been washing their nets when Jesus had asked to use the boat. Tending the nets was their last activity for the day; Peter had been fishing all night and was probably tired. In essence, Jesus was asking Peter to do something unexpected, something extra, and something that held little promise of success. He was asking Peter to believe that there were fish to catch during the day when he had just fished all night with no results.

Yet Peter accepted Jesus' invitation, and his resulting catch was so great that it nearly swamped the boat (see Luke 5:1–11).

The dream of parenting churches is the dream of doing something unexpected, something that requires extra effort, something that—some would say—holds little promise of success. It is a dream that involves investing people, finances, and resources into it. It is a dream that involves influencing an entire region through multiplication. Jesus invites us to dream of letting down our nets into deep water. If he has planted that dream in your heart, hold on to it, cultivate it. Write down the inner nudges that you feel. Ask God to clarify these promptings. Drive through your area envisioning the possibilities. Talk to church leaders who have parented or planted churches.

Then go—into the deep water—and let down your net for a catch.

PART 2

PREPARING TO PARENT CHURCHES

7 EMPOWERING NEW LEADERS

I served on the staff of Dr. John Maxwell at Skyline Wesleyan Church for six years. He shared with the staff a basic premise: everything rises and falls on leadership. This is true in every aspect of the church, but it is a very evident truth for parenting new churches. The leader must take responsibility for every area of the planting thrust. This does not mean that they are to do everything, but it means that they must be sure that everything is done.

Mike Regele cites the importance of leadership as a primary force in system creation in his book *Robust Church Development*. This book was written to help regional judicatories raise up and support missional faith communities within their denominations. Regele observes, "Success is dependent upon leadership that knows what it is doing and is capable of doing it."[1]

The challenge in many denominational structures is that they are led by managers. But leadership is not management.

"Management is primarily a maintenance function."[2] This statement made by J. Russell Crabtree in his challenging book *The Fly in the Ointment* is targeted at denominational leaders who are not genuinely serving their churches, not creating a strategy for change. "Leadership requires more than management. Leadership moves the Body forward; it catalyzes change."[3] And leadership is the catalyst that empowers and equips leaders and churches to multiply.

It takes a new breed of leader to participate in intentional church planting. It necessitates letting go of past paradigms. It demands that leaders build off their heritage but move into new realms of ministry. It takes those with an "Elisha spirit" to motivate a church-planting movement. An Elisha spirit is one that respects leaders who have gone before but is determined to move forward into the future. Elisha serves as an example of this kind of new leadership.

Elijah had served God and Israel for many years, and it was now time for him to step out of leadership. Elisha represents this new kind of leadership—a leadership that does ministry differently than its predecessors have done. Elisha's new leadership would reinvent ministry in such a manner that it would challenge a world different than that of Elijah. It was not Elijah's world any longer; it was Elisha's!

Elisha knew that he would need to do things differently than Elijah had. He did not simply want to recreate the ministry of Elijah, he wanted to exceed it. Elisha realized that to do Elijah's ministry again would impede the movement of God. Elisha's changes were not made in a spiteful, arrogant manner. Elisha simply understood that things do not stay the same. What it had taken to do ministry up to the point that he took over would no longer be required.

Those in leadership must sense their own call. Leaders must be convinced of their authority to lead their churches into multiplication. Leaders must escape the tyranny of tradition if they are to participate in a church-planting movement. Structural adjustments need to be made in order to accommodate the movement rather than adjusting the movement to accommodate a structure. Leaders must overcome their personal-style preferences if church-planting movements are to unfold. They must determine to empower this church-planting movement that is so necessary to infiltrating the culture. This will take missional leaders. Elisha is an example of just such a leader.

Elisha did four things that set the parameters for his ministry. If a church-planting movement is to be seen, led, participated in, and empowered, its leaders need to make the same four choices he did.

CONSIDER THE SITUATION

"Elisha left the oxen standing there, ran after Elijah, and said to him, 'First let me go and kiss my father and mother good-bye, and then I will go with you!' Elijah replied, 'Go on back, but think about what I have done to you'" (1 Kings 19:20). First, Elijah wanted Elisha to be aware of the price of leadership in the new era. This new responsibility was going to change everything for Elisha. The young man had been a farmer, and now he was going to be a prophet. He needed to give sincere consideration to the situation.

It takes a determined leader to move a church toward a multiplication mind-set. Churches are basically selfish. They tend to be inward-looking. A church-planting movement will not be spawned by inward-looking, self-absorbed churches. Many pastoral leaders find themselves in these kinds of churches, but they must understand that there will have to be a corporate mind-set change. Bob Roberts, founding pastor of Northwood Church near Fort Worth, Texas, says, "It isn't about us and our church but about Jesus and his church—and his church is far bigger than this one single church."[4]

FORFEIT COMFORT ZONES

"So Elisha returned to his oxen and slaughtered them. He used the wood from the plow to build a fire to roast their flesh. He passed around the meat to the townspeople, and they all ate" (1 Kings 19:21). Up to this point, Elisha had been a farmer. He had plowed the fields. He had done what he knew. Farming was his comfort zone. He knew plowing, but he did not know much about being a prophet. The second thing Elisha had to do was move from what he knew (his comfort zone) to that which he was not sure of. But Elisha made his choice. He killed the oxen and burned the plow. He could have put the plow into storage and the oxen out to pasture. If things did not work out, he could always go back to plowing. But he eliminated the temptation to go back, and he committed himself to moving forward into a new ministry.

Leading toward a church-planting movement means forfeiting comfort zones. For many this is counterintuitive to ministry training. It is doing church with a completely different methodology than they are used to. It is giving away resources, not gaining them. It is resisting the allure of what is big, bigger, biggest. It is a forfeiture of external measurements for eternal measurements.

Joel Comiskey places an emphasis on multiplying the church rather than merely growing a church larger: "To plant a church in every nation of the world requires a simple, reproducible strategy. It's not about growing a few churches larger and larger."[5]

FOLLOW THE CALL

"Then he went *with* Elijah" (1 Kings 19:21, emphasis added). Third, Elisha went with Elijah without condition. He did not require a guarantee of success. He did not demand a ministry description. He was not sure what this new calling would mean or where it might lead. He followed. It takes leaders of abandon to lead churches into church-planting movements.

Missional leaders will follow God's call regardless of where it takes them. They will follow even when there is a welling up of fear within them. They do this as they pursue the dream God has implanted in their heart. Theirs is a dream of a world changed by the gospel message.

BE AN UNRELENTING LEARNER

"[Elisha] went with Elijah as his *assistant*" (19:21, emphasis added). And fourth, Elisha was willing to learn. Missional leaders learn. They find mentors and models to help them find the way. They choose to be around those who will help them maximize their own potential—people whom they believe can grant them the double portion they will need to address the challenges and complications they will face in the future.

Today's missional leaders will need to learn new sets of skills, attitudes, and aptitudes. It takes a different skill set to raise up and empower leaders than it does simply to gather followers. Leadership development is necessary in order for a church to continue the expansion of God's kingdom and to birth church-planting movements. The skill set that is needed to develop leaders is driven by the attitude that followers do indeed become leaders, as in the case of Elisha and Elijah. The transition from being a follower to becoming a leader impacts future generations.

Tom Steffen, former church planter in the Philippines, speaks to the importance of passing off leadership: "Leaders who share their power with followers are actually setting the stage for developing new generations of leaders. Followers, by accepting a leader's influence will, over time, begin to change roles. That is, they will begin acting more and more like leaders themselves. Soon the follower will become a leader of a new group of followers. As leaders empower their followers the multiplication continues, creating new generations of leaders ready to carry on the vision of reaching a lost world for Christ."[6] Missional leaders who understand the importance of church-planting movements are needed to lead existing churches in multiplication.

It will be those leaders with an Elisha spirit who will transform churches into outwardly focused, culturally interactive centers. Leaders will lead by competency and character, not through control and command. It will be this kind of leader who God will use to impact the ever-changing landscape of North America in the twenty-first century.

8 EMBRACING KINGDOM EXPANSION

Church planting is kingdom expansion. Fred Herron makes clear that church planting is near to God's heart: "God has a heart for the expansion of his kingdom and a method for doing it: Planting local churches."[1] Roland Allen, missionary to China in the late nineteenth and early twentieth centuries, expands on this in his seminal work on the church's ability to expand spontaneously throughout its history: "This is what I mean by spontaneous expansion. I mean the expansion which follows the unexhorted and unorganized activity of individual members of the church explaining to others the gospel which they have found for themselves; I mean the expansion which follows the irresistible attraction of the Christian church for men who see its ordered life, and are drawn to it by desire to discover the secret of a life which they instinctively desire to share; I mean also the expansion of the church by the addition of new churches."[2] An expanding church, by definition, must start new churches.

Ed Stetzer and Warren Bird, in the summer 2008 edition of the *Journal of the American Society for Church Growth*, shared research on the state of church planting. Their study provided an overview of the starting of new churches in the United States. They identified the shared value of planting churches as kingdom expansion: "The value of church planting is expressed as the most effective means of evangelism that a church can participate in for the expansion of God's kingdom and the fulfillment of the Great Commission."[3]

Nina Beegle, editor of a small booklet called *Expanding Your Church's Mission* that was written for the church of the Nazarene, shares stories of how churches starting churches expanded their vision, impact, and effectiveness. Case after case reveals how churches that stepped out in faith and started a new congregation met an array of needs in their surrounding communities. In the booklet's foreword, Michael Estep states, "The explosive growth of our church in a number of our world areas is occurring because congregations see the importance of planting other churches."[4]

Writers and ministry practitioners, such as Neil Cole and Joel Comiskey, view small faith communities as essential for kingdom expansion. Cole's *Organic Church* highlights the fact that church multiplication is eased when structure is reduced and cultural connection is emphasized. "The Kingdom of God was always meant to spread spontaneously," says Cole. "It is viral in its organic approach infecting and transforming the nations."[5] This natural expansion is best realized when churches are birthed out of need and from evangelistic encounters. Comiskey highlights this trimmed-back method of multiplication: "The focus of the church is never the building but always the people. The true church consists of those who have placed their faith in Jesus Christ and live under his lordship."[6]

Church planters in England share this like-mindedness with Comiskey and Cole. The Crowded House Network of churches believes that lean and easily replicable churches are best for church expansion.[7] Tim Thornborough, contributor to *Multiplying Churches*, reveals how he implemented this model, and how such a model enhances evangelism: "The idea was to plant a church based on a model of the extended family, meeting in a house, and to set people free to spend time with and make friends with non-Christians. I wanted to work with a minimalist view of 'church' as a group of God's people gathered around his Word with a commitment to obeying it. This kind of church would involve no major capital outlay, no identifiable building, and with very few formal meetings. The clear focus was to be on evangelism."[8]

Reproductive churches are central to kingdom expansion. A variety of authors from diverse theological backgrounds view this principle as a core issue. Waldo Werning states, "Reproduction through multiplication is simply a life principle of all God-created organisms, including the church of Jesus Christ."[9] Charles Brock, one-time Southern Baptist missionary to the Philippines, observed, "Churches that produce new churches are a necessity; it is God's will. If this is an accepted fact, the church planter must think reproducible in every aspect of planting a church, from the time the first seed is sown to the actual birth of the church and as it continues to grow."[10]

Reproduction begins in the formative stage of a church and grows from there. Samuel Faircloth, in his book *Church Planting for Reproduction*, provides insight into the importance of building multiplication into a church's fabric. He states, "Reproduction must be built into the foundation of a new work."[11] In the same perspective Rodney Harrison, who wrote a practical guide for planting churches, believes church planting must be an ongoing activity for a new church, or the vision for it will quickly be lost.[12]

Tom Nebel and Gary Rohrmayer, in their classic book *Church Planting Landmines*, identify ten mistakes church planters need to avoid. Landmine number ten is delaying mission engagement. This problem, they say, is avoided by embedding multiplication into the core fabric of the church from its outset: "Leaders of new churches need to do whatever they can to imprint their church with a missional mind-set. The DNA is formed in the earliest days, and the opportunity to design your church into a kingdom-impact force will never be greater."[13]

Church planting is never easy. Its difficulty is amplified when a leader attempts to guide an already established church in multiplying other churches. Settled churches seem to resist this kind of multiplication. Aubrey Malphurs, who wrote a comprehensive guide for new churches, recognizes that "not many churches in America have taken the initiative to birth churches."[14] This reality appears to stem from a church's lack of wider vision, from its perspective that there are already enough churches, and from its unwillingness to release people to other works.

Existing churches need to see the benefit of starting new churches. God desires to have the gospel sown, and church planting is a key component of this sowing plan. Melvin Hodges sees church planting as God's plan: "God's program for today is a church planting program. He has indicated that he will accomplish his purposes for the world in this present epoch through the church."[15] Churches that participate in God's plan will plant churches.

In *Growing New Churches*, Carl Moorhous highlights the reward that church planting provides for a congregation that *mothers* a new church: "Planting a new church can be a richly rewarding experience for an established congregation. It can be the way for real growth, numerically as well as spiritually. It can with proper leadership, and devotion to Christ, lead the rooted congregation to greater spiritual heights, as they assist sacrificially their 'new-born' babe in the faith."[16] Highlighting the benefits of church planting to an established church may result in heightened interest by its church leadership in this kind of kingdom expansion.

Ralph Moore was an early adopter of this idea of churches planting churches. His book *Let Go of the Ring* tells the story of Hope Chapel. The story began in Hermosa Beach, California, when Moore had a vision to start a new congregation. That vision for one congregation became a vision for a multiplying congregation: "We pioneered churches from Hawaii to Montana to Texas. . . . Several of them started churches in neighboring localities."[17] Beyond encouraging church planting, Moore has been a tremendous advocate for churches spawning church-planting movements. In a conversation Ralph and I had, he shared with me that his church has over two hundred daughter churches now meeting as a result of their outreach that have in turn daughtered other churches.

Tom Nebel and Gary Rohrmayer clearly place churches planting churches as a catalyst for multiplication movements: "If your movement is going to move from addition to multiplication it will involve a clear strategy of encouraging local churches to engage in the parenting process of church planting."[18]

Bob Roberts, pastor of Northwood Church in Fort Worth, Texas, understands the power of church multiplication. In his book *The Multiplying Church*, he declares irrevocably, "Church planting is what *I* do. Church multiplication is what *we* do. Church planting is *my* story. Church multiplication is *our* story."[19] When leaders have this kind of view, it is clear that they have embraced the expansion of God's kingdom through church planting.

Roberts has bought into church planting full throttle. He undergirds the effectiveness of church planting when he says:

If I had to choose between starting ten churches that only grow to a hundred in a year or start one church that grows to a thousand in a year, I would prefer the ten churches with one hundred in attendance. Why? In time, many of those ten churches will surpass a thousand in attendance. If planting is in their DNA, in ten years they could have started fifty additional churches. What if they wound up only doing half of what we've done—that's 250 additional churches—and hopefully many of those will turn out to be church planting churches.[20]

Leader, what will you choose? Will you embrace church expansion? Will you get beyond the allure of building one church larger? Now is the time to extend God's kingdom through the starting of multiplying churches.

9 DETERMINING A PARENTING MODEL

There are two general types of church parenting: intentional and unintentional. There are examples of both types in Scripture, and either can result in a growing, healthy, and reproducing church.

The early church began in the city of Jerusalem, and the first believers might have stayed there if not for an unforeseen event: the persecution of the church. With the stoning of Stephen (see Acts 7), persecution broke out against the Christians in Jerusalem. As a result, the believers scattered. They moved across the Mediterranean region practicing this basic evangelistic principle: where we are is where we share. As they scattered, these Christians actually gathered a harvest of new believers who then needed new churches to nurture them and help them mature. These churches were started unintentionally.

Some scattered believers found themselves in Antioch (see Acts 11:19–21), and the local church they founded in that city ended up becoming an epicenter of multiplication. Once the church was begun, Barnabas brought Paul there to help with the local ministry. Later, the leadership of the Antioch church recognized the spiritual need of unreached people in the cities surrounding them, so they commissioned Paul and Barnabas to go on an evangelistic journey (see 13:1–3). Through this sending act, the Antioch church intentionally started a church-parenting movement.

In the twenty-first century, both unintended circumstances and intentional actions are still being used by God to parent new congregations. In our study, we will deal only with the intentional models.

INTENTIONAL PARENTING MODELS

Intentional parenting occurs when believers, prompted by the Holy Spirit, create a plan to initiate a new congregation. This merger of spiritual guidance and strategic planning probably creates the best circumstances for the birthing of a healthy reproducing congregation. Here are nine suggested models for intentional church parenting.

DAUGHTERING

When most people hear the word *Kleenex*, they think of a disposable facial tissue. To them that's what the word means. In fact, Kleenex is the trade name for one brand of facial tissues. *Xerox* is a similar term. To many the word *Xerox* means photocopy. But the word is really a trademark for one company that makes photocopy equipment. In the field of church parenting, the term *daughtering* has gained similar dominance. For many people that term is synonymous with the idea of church parenting, but daughtering is actually only one kind of church parenting.

Daughtering is when a single local church initiates and leads in the creation of a new congregation. In this model, the parent church assumes the primary responsibility for finding an individual to be the church planter (the new church's pastor), funding the project, and guiding the early stages of the new church's ministry. In the initial phases of the plant, the daughter church is often seen as an extension of the parent church's ministry. When this model is used, the parent church may receive assistance from a denomination or association, but the parent church has the responsibility for initiating and fulfilling the plans. Ideally, a daughter church would be encouraged to become a parent church itself once it is strong and healthy.

Foothills Community Church in Tucson, Arizona, had a vision to be a parenting church. Its leadership invited Pastor Dusty Farmer to join their staff as a church planter. He went to work raising up a core team from the parent church to help him plant a church in Sahurita, Arizona. This was a community about forty-five minutes southeast of the parent church.

In 2009 My Church of Sahurita was launched. My Church was begun with multiplication in their DNA. Only three years into their existence, God provided them with their own planter, Paul Santillo. So in 2012 My Church gave birth to Hilltop Community Church in Rio Rico, Arizona.

Foothills first gave birth to My Church. Then My Church gave birth to Hilltop. This is a marvelous example of both the daughter-church model and the expansion of the gospel through churches planting churches.

Just as Kleenex is only one type of facial tissue, daughtering is only one method of parenting a church. A true movement cannot be limited in its creativity.

SHARED PARENTING

Shared parenting is when two or more congregations work together to parent a church. The congregations combine their resources, but typically one of them takes the lead. This model is an outstanding option for smaller churches with limited resources or in an area in which several churches surround a strategic community.

SATELLITES

A satellite is an off-campus ministry begun by a local church with the eventual goal of the satellite becoming an organized, self-sustaining congregation. The satellite campus remains part of the parent church's organization until it is financially and organically strong enough to stand on its own. This model of parenting has a low impact on the mother church.

Mike Hilson of New Life Church in La Plata, Maryland, has done an excellent job of multiplication through satellite campuses. Real Life Church, Kneeling Point, and The Garage are three such satellites. Each of these churches share similar DNA, but they contextualize to the target audience they desire to reach.

MULTI-SITE

The multi-site model is similar to the satellite model but with one major difference: In the multi-site approach, there is no intention to form a new self-supporting church. The additional site (or sites) has its own leadership, pastor, and ministry emphasis, but it remains part of the parent church's structure. Typically, the campus pastors are staff members of the parent church.

New Hope Church in Durham, North Carolina, has adopted this approach. As of this writing, they have two sites functioning, with two more in the development stage. Pastor Benji Kelley is the primary preacher for each site. He is able to preach to both sites simultaneously through live video feed as well as by downloading messages from online. Frankly, this is not church parenting in the purest sense of the philosophy, but it is church multiplication. And more people are reached because they are not expected to arrive physically at the main campus.

A strong rural church might consider reaching surrounding communities via this model. Such congregations often already attract people from several small towns around them. A church might effectively reach those communities by beginning campuses in them.

LANGUAGE GROUP CONGREGATIONS

An existing church may parent a congregation by targeting a specific language group. Immigrants arrive in North America every day, many of whom have a desire to maintain their ethnic identity. Starting congregations for non-English speakers is a way to do cross-cultural ministry without ever leaving the country!

Faith Legacy Church in Sacramento, California, has provided space on its property for a Hispanic congregation to begin. Its staff provides resources, encouragement, and relationship for the Hispanic pastor. El Cajon Wesleyan outside San Diego, California, added an Iraqi pastor, Floreed Alaso, to their team. He began Maran Atha Ministry in the church's facility in order to reach the large population of Iraqi immigrants relocating to the East County of San Diego. Established churches are able to provide wombs for new churches if they see the potential in the non-English-speaking community.

HOUSE CHURCHES

A house church, as the name implies, is a church that meets in a private home. The house church model provides an excellent way to involve bivocational ministers or lay leaders in church planting. The cost of planting and maintaining a house church is minimal, and the potential for rapid multiplication is incredible.

House churches are not glorified Bible studies. They have the elements of a fully functioning body of believers. A house church is a group of believers committed to the Bible, to fellowship, to the breaking of bread, and to prayer, characteristics identified in Acts 2:42. The challenge of house churches for parenting churches and denominational entities is to allow a definition of church that will accommodate this new generation of children. Most house congregations will never become large or own property, but they can still function as viable local expressions of Christian fellowship, worship, and outreach. They hold the advantage of being highly relational and having a high degree of accountability.

A house church movement is in the embryonic stages in Lakeside, California. Under the leadership of Loren Holmquist, Rally Point Church has a vision to multiply dozens of house churches across the San Diego region. This church movement is being encouraged by Living Hope Christian Fellowship, also located in Lakeside.

ADOPTION

Occasionally, an independent group of worshipers looks for a place where they can find support and encouragement. Another local church may embrace such a group and help them establish leadership and organizational support. The daughter group already exists and is adopted by the parent church.

A group of second-generation Asian-Americans was meeting in a Bible study and had a vision to reach their network of acquaintances for Christ. They had come from a denomination that did not support them in fulfilling that vision. Leaders of this group approached a local church of another denomination and requested assistance. This local church adopted the small group of neighbors. The adoptive parent church helped the group find a pastor and gave them financial support and guidance to help them get established. Today this small Bible study has become a growing congregation committed to reproducing.

SURROGATE PARENTING

Surrogate parenting is a model for church planting in which the church plant is initially spearheaded by a denomination, association, or some other organization than a local church. A local church is then recruited to provide support for the new congregation. Four keys to successful surrogate parenting of a church are: (1) to establish clear roles for the district, the planter, and the surrogate parent; (2) to develop timeframes for recruiting core members as well as a target date for the new church to launch; (3) to negotiate accountability structures, clarifying who answers to whom; and (4) to communicate the benefits of being a surrogate parent.

NEXT PARADIGM

The next paradigm doesn't exist yet. It is an innovative model for church parenting that God is germinating in the heart of a church leader—maybe you. As church leaders gain a parenting mentality, more and more models for multiplying congregations will be developed. Only God knows where these innovations will take the church.

ART MORE THAN SCIENCE

Churches need to parent new churches. How it is done is not nearly as important as that it is done. I've heard it said that life isn't a science; we make it up as we go along. The same can be said for parenting churches. It is more of an art than a science.

When creating a work of art, the artist needs a medium (paint, lead, ink), a surface (canvas, paper, wall), and an applicator (brush, pen, airbrush). Each artist brings these elements together in a unique way. No two works of art are exactly the same.

Those who read these pages will come from different locations, situations, and backgrounds. In such a mix of people, circumstances, and challenges, there is an opportunity for each of us to create something unique—a new congregation. Each of us has the opportunity to use what we possess to meet the great need in the lives of people. Our canvases differ, but each one is ready to be covered with our God-given creativity and innovation.

There is no single right response to the challenge of parenting a new congregation. Let the Holy Spirit guide you in creating a work of art that brings glory to his name.

10 ADDRESSING THE BARRIERS OF CHURCH PLANTING

It wasn't big. It wasn't fancy. It wasn't in a great location. It wasn't all that expensive. It wasn't a lot of things. But the one thing it was made up for all it wasn't—it was ours! Joni and I had rented a number of apartments and various houses, and they had all been fine. They had provided adequate shelter, but we had never gotten terribly excited about them. On the day we moved into our own home, however, our attitude changed. We took pride in our home. We took special care of it. We had long-term plans for this house, and it showed. That shift in attitude is typical when people go from renting a home to owning one.

Something similar happens when people take ownership of nearly anything—including a vision for church parenting. Until pastors, board members, and other influence-makers in the local church own a vision for parenting, they will lack enthusiasm for expansion.

Rented vision is enthusiasm that is based on the desire or energy of another. When other leaders appear to be excited about church parenting, a not-so-enthused leader may feel some responsibility to support the effort. That support is usually nominal and short-lived, because those who rent the vision will always see church parenting as a mandate from outside the local church rather than as their own responsibility.

Rented vision usually results in empty words of affirmation and token financial support. Leaders with rented vision agree that there is a need for more churches, but they do not assume responsibility for creating them. Need alone does not create a burden in a leader's heart.

Multiplication happens when local congregations buy into the vision for church parenting. Ownership changes attitudes, availability, action—everything. So how is ownership of a vision created? What is the process by which local leaders purchase the vision of church planting for themselves? It begins with the pastor.

RELUCTANT LEADERSHIP

Without realizing it, a church's pastor may be the first obstacle to church multiplication. In the days when logs were floated downriver to a sawmill, the logs sometimes got tangled and clogged, causing a logjam. In many cases a logjam could be cleared by removing just one log. That log was the key to restoring movement. A novice logger would search for the source of the jam by going out on the river and jiggling logs until he found the key log. But this approach was time consuming and dangerous. A more experienced logger, however, would move away from the river's edge to a high spot of ground, a place from which he could survey the entire logjam. From that vantage point, the logger could see the key log; then he could go and move it. When the key log was moved, the entire flow followed.

When there is a barrier to casting a vision for church planting or parenting, the senior pastor is usually the key to resolving it. When he or she catches the vision, others follow. If the pastor is hesitant, the congregation will be too. Many pastors lack vision for church multiplication because they simply have never given the matter serious consideration. If that describes you, take the time to explore the church-planting movement. Give the mandate to reproduce churches due consideration before making up your mind about it. The first step in doing this is to seek God through prayer.

PRAY ABOUT CHURCH MULTIPLICATION

One of the clearest examples of leadership in the Bible is Nehemiah, who was used by God to lead the people of Israel in an aggressive renovation project. Nehemiah was the catalyst behind the Israelites' vision to rebuild the walls of Jerusalem. The Old Testament book of Nehemiah provides a study in the art of planning, leading, and managing change in the midst of adversity.

In the first four verses of Nehemiah 1, we discover the secret of this man's leadership: He got on his knees. Prayer is the secret to success in any kingdom endeavor. The first step in exploring the possibility of church parenting is to go before God and ask, "What, if anything, do you want me to do in this area?"

The problem confronting Jerusalem was one of security. The city's walls had been broken down and its gates burned with fire (see Neh. 1:3). This was no condition for a city, but was it Nehemiah's problem? Remember that need alone does not constitute a burden. Jerusalem's need for security did not automatically become Nehemiah's responsibility. He didn't even live in Jerusalem. In fact, he had never been there. He had a good position serving the king of a distant land. Things for him were running smoothly. Finances were adequate. Why would Nehemiah spend time and energy on a community in which he had little personal investment? Besides, Nehemiah was a cupbearer by training, something like a food service manager. He wasn't a builder.

As pastors, we often find ourselves in situations similar to Nehemiah's. We are fulfilled in our ministries; things are going well. We're good at what we do and busy with the affairs of our local church. The people in our congregations are being challenged and changed. So why bother doing something (church parenting) that we've never been trained to do in a place to which we've never been? While acknowledging the need for more churches, a pastor may well ask, "What does that have to do with me?"

Nehemiah's response to Jerusalem's broken-down state was to pray about the situation. He wrote, "When I heard these things [the condition of Jerusalem], I sat down and wept. For some days I mourned and fasted and prayed before the God of heaven" (1:4 NIV). It's interesting that Nehemiah didn't immediately jump on the go-rebuild-Jerusalem bandwagon. Nor did he simply dismiss the situation as none of his concern. He fasted and prayed. His decision—whatever it would be—would be made on his knees. His reaction to the need would not be based on his personal goals, his "ministry wedge," or his preferred geographic location. It would be based on prayer. The story that takes place in the book of Nehemiah is birthed in 1:4, in which we see Nehemiah's prayer.

It is true that need alone does not constitute a burden, yet many pastors never even enter a discussion about church parenting as a potential answer to the needs around them. Church leaders tend to either dive into the church multiplication wave or jump out of its way. Maybe it's time to discuss the matter with the one whose opinion matters most—God. As leaders, we need to enter God's presence and honestly seek his direction. As Floyd Tidsworth puts it, "Prayer should saturate the whole effort of starting a church."[1]

If you've never seriously considered the idea of church parenting, I urge you to do so. Get out your smartphone, tablet, or whatever you use to track appointments, and locate a day in the next two weeks on which you have a minimum of four hours available. Block out that time to spend in seeking the will of God. Go to a place where you will have no interruptions. Take a Bible and something to write with, but leave your cell phone at home. Spend the time reading the book of Acts and asking God for wisdom. Focus on this question: "Lord, what, if anything, do you want me to do in the area of church multiplication?"

SET ASIDE DEFINITIONS OF "SUCCESS"

In order to give church multiplication fair consideration, pastors must learn to think beyond the traditional measures of success used in the church. Success tends to be measured by three Bs: buildings, bodies, and budgets. In each of these areas, a church's goal is to have more. The perceived value of these measures is underscored by the applause and attention given to pastors of larger churches. Most pastors, regardless of the size of their church, eventually come to feel that they must produce an ever-larger congregation in order to be successful in the ministry.

There is nothing inherently wrong with wanting to build a great church for God, even if that greatness is measured by the three Bs. But the kingdom of God cannot be bound by a church's property line. Pastors whose desire for church growth becomes a fixation in their own ministry will inevitably concentrate their work on one church in one place instead of parenting multiple churches in multiple locations.

Dr. Mark Williams of Dynamic Church Planting International once told me, "Churches that plant churches need a pastor with a real vision for the lost and a complete lack of selfishness."[2] It takes an unselfish leader to look beyond one's own church. It takes an unselfish leader to invest people and resources into a ministry from which the leader's own congregation may not benefit directly. Pastor, open your mind to the possibility that your greatest success may be your investment in the ministry of others. Allow yourself to break free from the confining notion that your building, attendance average, and budget are the only measures of your effectiveness. Take time to get on your knees and seek God; open yourself to his leading and prompting. You are the key to creating a vision for church multiplication within your congregation.

THE COST OF INVESTING

I am not a financial wizard. I don't track the stock market. My few investments are in mutual funds, and I pretty much leave them alone. But even I know that it is better for investments to increase in value rather than to decrease. No one would intentionally place money in a portfolio, knowing that their action would result in a loss. In the same way, many pastors are slow to adopt the idea of church parenting—they see it as a loss for their congregations.

Church parenting is costly, but its cost is an investment, not a loss. There is a cost to investing in the stock market, but those who buy stocks are not throwing away money. Their goal is to get a return. They hope to make money, not lose it. In the same way, church parenting is an investment in the kingdom. Churches that parent other churches do not lose. They do not lose money; they invest it into a situation that will result in a net return to the kingdom. They do not lose people; they invest them in the work of gathering a harvest. Is that mere semantics? No. It is a difference in mind-set, a difference in attitude. If a local church views church planting as a loss to itself, it will never embrace a parenting project. To successfully multiply, a congregation must view church parenting as an investment in the kingdom.

When Arcade Wesleyan Church, the church I pastored from 1994 to 2000 in Sacramento, California, parented its first daughter church, we invested fifty-five people in the church plant. This was roughly 15 percent of our Sunday morning congregation. Occasionally, people who remained at Arcade would say, "We lost some of our key people!" But I would put up my hand to keep them from going on, then correct them by saying, "We didn't lose them; we invested them. The kingdom will get a return." Soon we began to laugh about it. When chatting about the church plant, people would catch themselves starting to say "lost" and quickly change to "invest." I caught myself doing it on several occasions.

What investment is required of a parent church? There are five resources that a congregation must be willing to part with in order to parent a church. I call them the five Ms.

MEMBERS

A parent church may need to invest members in a church plant. Many people who are active in congregational life will respond to the opportunity to help establish a new congregation. Often, these volunteers will be the cream of the crop. Why do the best and the brightest respond to challenges? They have a high degree of buy-in to the church's mission, and they have a "Bring it on!" mentality.

Core members of a congregation are the first to buy into the vision of church planting because they want to expand their church's ministry influence. They recognize right away that church parenting is central to the work of the kingdom, and they want to support it. They see church parenting as part of the mission of the local church. These people typically have the attitude of Caleb, who said confidently to Joshua, "Give me the hill country" (Josh. 14:12). They want to explore new ministry territory and are prepared to be uncomfortable for God.

Mark was a board member and a lead Sunday school teacher at Arcade Wesleyan Church. I'd had the privilege of discipling him, and he'd been in an accountability group with me for four years. He was a leader, and he was a friend and confidant of mine. Standing in the church parking lot one day, he told me that he and his wife Danielle were going to help begin Spring Valley Church, Arcade's third parenting effort. I can still hear his exact words: "This is the right thing to do. Besides, I am ready for a new challenge."

Quality leaders are always ready to go and to be used, and we must let them go. To be successful in church parenting, we must be willing to release key church members into the care of another. It is never easy, but it is right. Don't be selfish. Hold your church's human resources loosely. Be willing to invest them in the kingdom.

Sometimes I'm asked, "Have you had disgruntled people leave your church to join a church planting effort?" My honest, yet tongue-in-cheek, response is, "No, unfortunately!" Church parenting does not clear the deadwood from a congregation; it gives away a church's best fruit. Disgruntled members will stay and continue to be your humbling agent. May God bless you both.

Of course, not all the best people will leave a church to join a church parenting team. Some will stay. God lays on the hearts of many the call to remain at the parent church and to strengthen it. In 2000 Jim Bogear planted The River Church in Sacramento as a daughter of Arcade Wesleyan Church. When he began to recruit the core team from Arcade, he helped the congregation understand the call of planting. He let it be known that the call was for everyone. God calls some to go and grow a new church; he calls others to stay and stabilize the parent. Regardless, they are all called!

Keep looking for those who can be developed into leaders. Cultivate people intentionally and regularly. Create leadership incubators to nurture potential leaders. All leaders in the church should recruit and develop others so that there will be someone to fill their shoes if they are called to step out into a new venture.

MONEY

A parent church invests money in its daughter from two sources: the tithe of the core team members and parental gifts.

When people are invested in a new church venture, their giving goes with them. The tithes of these core team members provide the new church its initial financial footing. Never does a church live more on the ragged edge of faith than when it risks its finances. It is interesting that we tell individuals to trust God in their personal finances, but we quiver at the prospect of trusting God corporately. Do we really believe what we preach?

In one of the churches that I helped launch, two of the top five financial contributors to the parent church were called to go to the new one. One was the single largest giver, an entrepreneurial businessman. He not only gave regularly throughout the year, but also provided the church a special year-end gift. He was a board member, a leader, and a person of influence. Honestly, investing his influence and leadership into the new venture didn't concern me as much as our church losing his financial contribution. When I first discovered that he and his family were called to go with the daughter church, I asked God, "OK, how are you going to pull this off?"

Within one week, I received a phone call from a young couple. A few months earlier, I'd had the privilege of helping Diane back to the Lord and leading her husband Jeff into a relationship with Jesus. They had been attending our church for less than six months. They asked to see me that day, and an hour later they were seated in my office.

"I've been listening to your sermons on tithing," Jeff began, "and we want to do that. How do we start?"

I reminded them what tithing was, explained how to use the church's offering envelopes, and suggested that Sunday morning would be a good time to begin giving.

"We want to start that now," Jeff said, and he meant it. He opened his checkbook, wrote a check, placed it in one of the offering envelopes I'd given him, and handed it to me. I was startled by their passion but had enough presence of mind to pray with them before they left. Later I glanced at the outside of the envelope. The amount they had given was significant, and I thought they might have made a mistake. Although I wouldn't normally do this, I decided to open the envelope to be sure the amount was correct. It was. Obviously, this couple was making up for lost time and giving several weeks' worth of tithe at once.

While their contribution did not replace that of the two families who were joining the daughter church, God used the occasion to remind me that he would provide for all our needs. Perhaps it would take several families to replace the two that were leaving, but then, God had provided those families to us in the first place—they were not mine to hold. As ministry leaders, our job is to release resources; it is God's job to replenish them.

MUD

A parent church invests turf and territory—mud—into a daughtering effort. It's tempting to become arrogant and territorial in the ministry. We are arrogant to believe that only we can reach the community around us. We are territorial when we think that no other church should encroach on our "God-given" area. Never mind that we have had many years to reach those around us and have not done it effectively.

There is nothing wrong, of course, with believing that you have a wonderful church and that everyone should want to attend it. I have always felt that way about my own local church. But not everyone attends my church, and that fact will never change. Church parenting acknowledges the fact that no one church will reach an entire community. We need a variety of churches to reach a variety of people.

Invest mud. Release territory. My friend Dr. Mark Williams emphasized the need for this kind of generosity when he told me, "A pastor has to gain a kingdom mind-set, a belief that the Lord is pleased with the harvest, even if it isn't in his own fields."

MINISTRY RESOURCES

A parent church invests ministry resources in its daughter— the gifts, skills, and talents of the people whom they invest. People cannot go and leave their abilities behind. The good news is that God will raise up others in the parent congregation to meet its ministry needs. It's likely that they will be unexpected people whom God is even now grooming to fill the gaps left by others. Their gifts and skills will be manifested as they sense the call to stay and strengthen the parent.

It's like having a bullpen—the stable of relief pitchers on a baseball team. God holds people in reserve until just the right time. When relief is needed, he calls them out. Release your ministry resources. God will draw upon his bullpen to meet your need. Your team is deeper than you might think.

MOMENTUM

It would be a mistake to sugarcoat the cost of investing in a new church. The parent church must also sacrifice momentum in order to create a daughter congregation. The parent congregation will gear down. When members, money, mud, and ministry resources are invested, there will be a lag in the parent church's momentum. That natural phenomenon results from two contrasting feelings among the parent congregation. The first is incredible joy; the second is sorrow.

The joy comes from realizing, "We did it! God used us to begin a new work. Many people will be reached because of our investment. Our influence is expanding into areas we never dreamed possible." Just as a sports team savors winning a championship, a parent church should bask in the parenting of a healthy church. There should be time for celebrating victories. Yet there will be a lull in the church's momentum even as the sweet success is enjoyed.

The second reaction is sorrow. That comes from the realization, "We did it! We parented this church! We invested friends and family to make it happen. There are faces we will not see for some time. Our relationships will change. They will be a part of us, but they will be apart from us." Just as a new mother can feel postpartum sadness along with excitement about the birth of her baby, a mother church feels sorrow about the loss and change in their midst along with joy over the daughter's birth. Every church must process that sadness, first by acknowledging it. Feelings of loss do not negate the joy of the parenting. Second, every congregation needs time to recover from the stress of parenting a church. It must rest and focus on growing stronger. The week after launching a daughter church is not the time to introduce a multiphase building program. But these mixed emotions will pass.

THE GOD GAP

Parenting a church will stretch a congregation as few other things will, because it forces a church into the God gap—the place where our resources stop and God's must start. Parent churches dwell in the God gap.

Peter became a walking—and drowning—illustration of the God gap when he stepped out to meet Christ on the water. Peter began within the comfortable confines of the boat; but when he saw Jesus walking on the water, Peter wanted to join the Lord. As soon as Peter swung his leg out of the boat, his resources were exhausted. He needed God's help if he was to succeed.

When you make the decision to parent a new congregation, you step over the side of the boat. It's a scary moment, fraught with the potential for failure. But like Peter, you will have entered the God gap, that place where you can experience the touch of Jesus as never before. Are you ready? Step into the gap.

11 AVOIDING MYTHS, HINDRANCES, AND HURDLES

The rock has been thrown. The ripple is expanding. All appears to be well, until you realize that something is impeding the ripple's progress. You were so focused on the point of impact that you did not notice the logs, fallen trees, and bushes that might hinder the wave's advancement. This debris impedes the motion of the expanding ripples. Will it halt the movement altogether?

It doesn't have to. When ripples in a pond encounter some disruption, they don't stop—they go around it. The ripple created by church multiplication is likely to encounter some obstacles, but they need not stop its progress. As a leader, you can minimize the effect of these negative factors if you recognize them, understand them, and are prepared to deal with them.

There will always be myths, hindrances, and hurdles regarding church parenting. Remove them, however, and you will increase the likelihood that your ripple will expand to the other shore.

MYTHS TO EXPOSE

Myths are false notions that are commonly accepted as true. For example, many of us were taught that George Washington once threw a dollar across the Potomac River. Although that never happened, many people continue to believe that the story is true. A number of myths surround the church-multiplication movement. These are fundamental misunderstandings of what is involved in a successful church-parenting effort. These false notions have dissuaded many from attempting church planting or parenting. Here are four of the most common church parenting myths.

THE MYTH OF ATTENDANCE

The myth of attendance is the misconception that a congregation must be a certain size to successfully parent a church. Most local church leaders who resist church parenting believe that their church is either too small, too large, or too mid-sized to parent another church. Whatever their size, most church leaders believe it is the wrong one.

Yet parenting has little to do with a church's attendance; it depends much more on the church's attitude. It's not the size of the congregation but the size of its heart that counts. You can probably name an undersized athlete who excelled in spite of her small stature. "She's got heart!" is what we often say about such overachievers. Any church, large or small, that has a heart for reaching the lost can find the means to become involved in church parenting.

Pastors sometimes claim—perhaps as a way of putting off the issue—that they will attempt church parenting when their own congregation reaches a certain size. They rarely do, however, because church parenting is not in their hearts. These pastors are like church members who claim that they will begin tithing when their income reaches a certain level. These members seldom follow up on their claims, because the issue is not their cash flow but their attitude about stewardship. In the same way, churches that have no heart for multiplication when they are small seldom acquire one as they grow larger.

But is there an optimum size for church parenting? Some church-planting consultants believe that congregations averaging from one hundred to five hundred in attendance are the best size to parent a church. My own experience confirms that. Churches in that size-range generally have the resources to parent and are usually not encumbered with debt. That puts them in an ideal position to invest people in a new venture yet retain a critical mass.

That ideal range should not be taken as a firm boundary, however. Is there an ideal size for a wide receiver in the National Football League? Yes, but there are many accomplished receivers who don't fit the ideal profile. Churches of all sizes can participate in parenting.

THE MYTH OF AGE

Some leaders wrongly believe that only churches of a certain age can successfully parent a congregation. They have in mind the age of the institution, not the age of its members. Usually, such leaders believe that their church is too old to undertake a parenting project. Like a woman who believes that her "biological clock" has stopped ticking, some pastors think that even if they wanted to produce a daughter congregation, it's too late — their church is too old now.

It is true that a church is most apt to parent in its first three years of existence. That's because newer churches tend to be more adaptable. Younger churches have fewer traditions to contend with and no sacred cows to overcome. That is one reason, by the way, why it is so important to implant the idea of multiplication into the thinking—the DNA—of a daughter church. When a church is planted with the expectation that it will become a parent and then held accountable to that expectation, the results are powerful.

Yet the fact that young churches reproduce more readily than do older ones does not mean that older congregations cannot or should not become involved in church multiplication. Older congregations often have more resources than younger ones. Youth has exuberance, but maturity has stability. Older congregations lend credibility to a movement. Regardless of their age, churches can multiply.

THE MYTH OF ACQUISITION

The myth of acquisition holds that a church must achieve certain goals for itself before it will be in a position to parent a congregation. That notion is revealed in statements like these:

- "We will start a new congregation after our building project is completed."
- "Once we've added a couple staff members, we'll be in a position to try this."
- "If we can increase our budget to this amount, we'll try a church plant."

These churches always seem to have one more thing on their to-do list. Somehow they never quite get around to parenting a new congregation.

It isn't either/or. Churches do not have to choose between growing their own ministries and planting new churches. They can do both. After developing a willingness to invest outside themselves, most churches discover that they regain whatever they let go. They gain new converts, members, finances, and energy. Local growth is not the motivation for church parenting, but it can be a wonderful side effect.

THE MYTH OF ADEQUACY

I was sitting across the table from the pastor of a growing church in a metropolitan area. Over the years he had led his congregation as it grew from a handful of people to more than two thousand. Now he had a vision to parent three churches over the next five years. Although he was a proven leader with an excellent record, he confessed, "I have no idea how to go about this." Fortunately, that didn't hinder him from moving forward.

The myth of adequacy holds that church leaders must be experts in the art of church multiplication in order to become involved in church parenting. Some leaders use their lack of know-how as an excuse for not parenting. It is a poor excuse, though, given the ready availability of church-planting consultants and tools. Resources are available. Churches at all levels of understanding can participate in a parenting effort. Lack of expertise should not be a barrier to involvement.

Which of these four myths have prevented you from considering church parenting? Which do you hear most commonly among members of your congregation? How might you respond to them now that you recognize them as false? Nearly every church can become involved in the church-multiplication movement. No church should be left behind.

HINDRANCES TO AVOID

I pulled out of my driveway one day and began driving toward my office. As I drove along, my car seemed to labor more than usual. I sensed some resistance in the vehicle, almost as if something was holding me back. I continued along my way, but I knew that something wasn't right. After driving a couple of miles, I discovered that I had forgotten to release the parking brake. It's amazing how much easier a car moves when its brakes are off!

There are several hindrances that can put the brakes on a church-planting movement. Like an engaged parking brake, they will not keep the movement from progressing, but they will cause it to labor unnecessarily. When you understand these hindrances, it is much easier to cast them off and continue moving freely. Here are seven hindrances to church parenting—and how to avoid them.

FOCUSING ON HEALTH FOR HEALTH'S SAKE

In recent years, there has been a shift in emphasis from church growth to church health. Much of the credit for that is due to the incredible work of Christian Schwarz in his book *Natural Church Development*. Health is a crucial characteristic for a successful parent church, and healthy churches are more likely to participate in church multiplication. Yet health may become a hindrance to church parenting when a church focuses on health for health's sake. Some congregations become virtual hypochondriacs, monitoring their health so closely that they are unwilling to do anything else. Truly healthy churches are not self-focused. A byproduct of their healthy condition is a willingness to invest energy in others.

A WELFARE MENTALITY

Some church leaders resist planting new churches because they want to help existing churches that are not doing well. "Why use our money to start new churches?" they wonder. "Don't we have an obligation to help the churches we already have?"

The root of this thinking is the notion that money will solve any problem. Denominations and associations that continue to pour money into struggling or dying churches unwittingly create a welfare mentality. The result is that problems are perpetuated rather than alleviated. Struggling churches seldom lack money alone. While it is true that the need to plant new churches does not preempt the need to help existing ones, it is equally true that the need of a struggling congregation does not nullify the mandate to create new, healthy churches. To liberally paraphrase Jesus, "Struggling churches you will always have with you" (see Matt. 26:11).

TERRITORIALISM

Planting new churches is sometimes perceived as an infringement on the territory of others who are trying to reach a given community. Squatters may not be welcomed.

Yet there are more people in any community than any one church can reach. Usually existing churches in a given location have had decades—even centuries—to evangelize their communities. New churches will reach people that these existing congregations never have and perhaps never will. It is a mistake to put the needs of lost people on hold until existing churches find the right time and the right program to reach them.

THE "FILL 'ER UP" MIND-SET

I lived through the gas crisis of the 1970s, as did millions of others. During that time, many gas stations were open only on certain days. In some places, cars with even-numbered license plates could buy gas on some days and those with odd-numbered plates on other days. Long lines at filling stations were common, and many drivers became worried when their gas gauges dipped below half a tank. When it was my day to fill up, I did not like to see other cars at the filling station. After all, they were after the same limited resource that I needed.

Some leaders bring a similar mind-set to the discussion of church multiplication. They want to see existing churches filled before adding new ones. "When the churches we have are bursting at the seams," they reason, "we'll consider planting new ones."

That never happens, of course. We will never fill up all the existing churches in any denomination or in any community. The best way to increase our capacity is to add more containers, not to fill existing ones to the brim. We must not allow an unreachable goal (filling all existing churches to capacity) to hinder us from pursuing an achievable one (planting new churches).

DOING WHAT GETS REWARDED

When I served on John Maxwell's staff at Skyline Wesleyan Church, he told staff members, "What gets rewarded is what gets done." This is true in all organizations, including denominations. What gets rewarded in most denominations is a church's increase in the three Bs: buildings, bodies, and budgets. Churches that are increasing in attendance, adding staff or facilities, or gaining income are singled out for applause. In spite of a growing emphasis on church health, growth is still the goal for churches among leaders of most denominations. We reward pastors who are able to gather more people at one place at one time.

The urge to do what gets rewarded is a hindrance to church multiplication, because church parenting is not on the applause list for most denominations. Often denominations even place unintentional barriers in the path of parent churches. For instance, churches that undertake a local building project may be allowed to pay a reduced amount in denominational support for a period of time, but such incentives are seldom offered to churches that undertake a parenting project. The not-so-subtle message in this is that denominations value real-estate construction but not church multiplication.

Leaders who become involved in church multiplication must shake off the temptation to do only what gets rewarded. Their ultimate motivation is found in the Lord's words, "Well done, my good and faithful servant" (Matt. 25:21, 23). However, a human pat on the back doesn't hurt as we move toward the heavenly standing ovation. When denominations or organizations begin to applaud—and financially back—congregations that choose to multiply, more churches will get involved in church parenting.

FEAR OF RESPONSIBILITY

Maternity wards are full of life, but they are also full of challenges. Babies are messy. They bring both lots of joy and lots of hard work. As they grow, children both delight and disturb their parents. New churches are much the same. Many congregations resist parenting because they don't want to deal with the mess, work, or frustration of bringing new life into the world. Leaders must overcome the fear of responsibility—both in themselves and in their congregations—in order to successfully parent a new church.

AVOIDING RISK

Church planting will never have a 100 percent success rate. Some new congregations won't make it. Church leaders generally realize that and often fear the possibility of failure. Why put so much effort into something that may not work? But all worthwhile endeavors carry some risk. Church planting is both worthwhile and risky. Where there is fear, the best response is faith. Leaders must be willing to risk their resources—and their reputations—and then trust God for the results.

Hindrances should not be dismissed; they must be addressed. Like parking brakes, these hindrances have a legitimate function— they raise appropriate cautions. When I discovered that my parking brake was still engaged, I didn't disassemble it. I merely disengaged it, because it was not useful at that point in my journey. Understand and recognize the attitudes described here. Allow them to be appropriate cautions, but never let them become hindrances to the work that God wants to do in your region through you.

HURDLES TO CLEAR

I was on the track-and-field team in high school, and I competed in the heavy events of shot put and discus. A friend of mine competed in the low and high hurdles. One day at practice, I asked him for a quick lesson. He gave me a few tips, and I gave hurdling a try. The result wasn't good, however. In fact, I am lucky to be here to write about it! My inexperience in knowing how to navigate the hurdles resulted in pain both physical (from hitting them) and emotional (from the laughter of friends). That experience convinced me that I would make an excellent shot putter.

An experienced hurdler, however, can clear those obstacles gracefully, almost effortlessly. When a person understands the technique and has some experience with it, hurdles aren't so difficult to overcome. That's true in church parenting as well. There are hurdles, obstacles to success. If you hit them unprepared, pain is the likely result. With a little training, though, you can clear them gracefully.

FEAR

Church parenting may cause two types of fear. The first is internal. It manifests itself in questions about the parent church's ability to invest in the project and to recover from it. Will the parent continue to grow? Will it be healthy? The second fear is external and raises questions about the daughter congregation. Will the new church make it? Will it grow and be healthy? I vividly remember lying awake the night before my oldest child's first day of school. I couldn't sleep as I worried whether I had done all I could to prepare him for the rigors of kindergarten. It was heartrending. A parent church may experience that same kind of anxiety for its child.

These fears are natural, but they should not form a barrier to church parenting. They can be overcome by courage and faith. I like the statement "When fear knocks at the door, let faith answer." The fear of parenting is real, but we can step over it.

FINANCES

Financing church plants will be dealt with in detail in a later chapter, but I mention it here because it is a hurdle that must be crossed. Leaders must identify and cultivate income streams that will support the parenting effort. The problem really concerns creativity more than finances. Churches find the money to do what they value. Financing is an issue that must be addressed, but it should not become a barrier to participation in church multiplication.

PERSONALITY SHIFT

A church's personality results from the collective spirit of those whom God has placed within its walls. So when a congregation invests people in a church plant, the parent church's personality shifts. This can disrupt the congregation, but it does not necessarily bring a negative result.

The minister of music in the church I most recently pastored felt called to plant a church. When he left, our worship team remained intact. We had the same keyboard player, drummer, lead guitarist, and vocalists. The quality of the music remained strong, as well. But the feel was different. The church had to adjust to this shift in personality.

Changes in the parent church's personality can be challenging, but they are certainly not life-threatening. Treat them as hurdles to be overcome with energy and spirit.

DENOMINATIONAL PERCEPTION

In my denomination, pastors and lay leaders gather for an annual district conference at which we celebrate the previous year's achievements. One of the report systems we use is a graph that shows the growth pattern for each church in our district. When a church invests people and resources into a daughter church, there is an excellent chance that the graph will show a downturn. To those who don't know—or don't care—that the church has invested itself in multiplication, it will appear that the church is unhealthy. Why else would people leave the congregation?

Overcoming the hurdle of misperception requires inner strength. Church leaders must be more convinced that their investment in parenting is worthwhile than they are concerned about their reputation among their peers. A ripple church must be self-confident. It must accept the fact that other leaders may not value what it is doing.

TIMING

Timing is everything. The timing of a comment from one spouse to another can make the difference between a good discussion and a heated argument. Timing can also make the difference between an effective church plant and a failed effort.

The first daughter church that I was involved in creating was launched four months before the original target date. As our church worked toward the launch date, the planter and I realized that the parent was more prepared for this birth than we had anticipated. We realized that waiting for an artificial launch date would hinder our momentum, so we elected to launch early. The church had a successful launch, partly due to the timing.

Bad timing can interrupt a ripple movement more than any other hurdle. When the time for action is right, the ripple flows evenly across the lake. When the timing is wrong, a ripple is unable to progress much beyond the point of impact. An ill-timed plant can dishearten a congregation and dissuade it from planting again. People will point to the failed experience as the reason a church should never again involve itself in planting. The better the timing, the better the results; the better the results, the better the chance of a congregation parenting again.

PEACE OF MIND

My wife's phone call was terse and to the point. "You need to get home. Ryan has fallen off his scooter, and he has a gash in his arm. I can't calm him down—he needs to get to the emergency room."

Fortunately, the church was near our home, so I was able to get to my family quickly. When I arrived, my then-seven-year-old son was in our front yard in hysterics. He wanted no one near him. He knew he was hurt, but fear was the only medicine he would accept. I stepped toward him and began talking to him soothingly. Once in range, I grabbed him in my arms, and he began to settle down.

We got in the car and headed toward the emergency room. Joni drove, and I sat in the passenger seat with Ryan on my lap, holding him close to my chest. I was nearly as hysterical on the inside as Ryan was on the outside, but I found the composure to calmly explain what he would soon experience in the emergency room. I told him about the registration process at the hospital. I described how we would go into a curtained room and be seated on a gurney with other sick people nearby. I explained that the doctor would give him a shot, which might hurt a little but would take away the pain in his arm. I did my best to tell him about how the doctor would clean the wound and stitch his arm. I did everything I could think of to prepare him for the experience he was about to face. "You can handle this," I told him. "It's going to be all right."

It worked. By the time we arrived at the hospital, Ryan was calm. His medical treatment went more or less as I had described, and he took it like a champ. Heightening his awareness of what was to come did much to soothe his nerves and to make the entire process go smoothly.

In the same way, understanding the potential myths, hindrances, and hurdles to church parenting will demystify the process and help a church to navigate it calmly and successfully. When we know what's ahead, we will be prepared to meet it.

It's going to be all right. This is something you can do.

ACTING AT THE RIGHT TIME   12

When Joni and I got married, I was only halfway through my undergraduate degree. I still had lots of schooling before me. I was facing two more years of undergraduate work and then three years of graduate school. My wife and I decided not to have children until I completed my education. We felt this would be best for us relationally, economically, and professionally. Our plan worked out well. I completed my master's degree in June 1980, and our first child was born in September of that year.

There was never any question about whether we would become parents. We knew that having children was something we wanted to do. But the timing was an issue. We wanted to provide the best possible environment for our children. Frankly, I'm not sure we were totally prepared when we had our first son, but we were more prepared than we would have been before.

Timing is an important consideration when parenting churches. Some times are better for parenting than others. Of course, no congregation will ever feel completely ready to become a parent church. The goal is to identify the optimum time, not the perfect time. So how will you know when your church is ready to parent? What is the optimum time to get involved in church multiplication?[1]

POSITIVE INDICATORS

I have provided seven indicators that will help leaders identify their congregation's readiness to parent a church. These indicators have nothing to do with the number of buildings a church owns, the number of members it has, or the size of its budget. Instead, they point to the presence of the attitude and atmosphere within the church. It is not necessary to have all seven indicators in order to launch a church multiplication project. Any one of these may provide enough capital to motivate a congregation to begin the parenting journey.

A BURDEN FOR LOST PEOPLE

Any congregation that has the desire to see people brought into the kingdom has the potential to become a parent. Church planting is the most effective method of evangelism. If a church has the heart to be a vehicle for the salvation of others, it should build church parenting into its strategic plan. Parenting is as essential a tool for winning people to Christ as are the methods of personal soul winning, door-to-door evangelism, acts of compassion, and programmed attraction events. A church that wants to reach the lost can become a parent church.

A WILLINGNESS TO STEP OUT IN FAITH

We must take a step of faith in order to enact any vision. Many churches regularly display a willingness to do this. How do we know if a church is ready to undertake a parenting project? We need to ask a few questions: Has the church committed surplus income to missions? Has it brought on a staff person in anticipation of growth? Have its members given above and beyond their tithes to build a building or purchase property? All these actions are attempts to enact a vision—to make what is unseen become a reality. They are steps of faith. A church that is willing to attempt the unseen has the potential to be a parenting church.

A VISION FOR REGIONAL INFLUENCE

In chapter 5, I made the distinction between a regional church and a regional ministry. A regional ministry recognizes that not everyone in a given area will attend one church in one location. The largest churches in the world do not reach every person in their communities, much less in their regions. They may have outstanding programs that attract a large number of people, but there are even more people that they will never reach.

A church that understands this concept has the potential to become a parent church. Does your congregation realize that it can multiply its effectiveness by extending its ministry beyond its property line? Does the church want to reach beyond its community into the surrounding region? If so, it may be ready for church parenting.

A SPIRITUAL MATURITY

It takes mature, unselfish people to parent churches. A spiritually mature congregation is one that is growing in its understanding of the Word and of the Word's application to life. A congregation that is growing in Christ will hunger to multiply. The tug of the Spirit will draw it to spread the gospel, both individually and corporately. A church that is increasing its spiritual depth has the potential to be a parenting church.

A GENEROUS SPIRIT

A congregation that is generous toward its pastoral staff, guest speakers, missionaries, surrounding community, and neighboring churches displays a key indicator of its readiness to become a parent church. Church parenting is an act of generosity. God gives us resources so that we might be generous with them. In his letter to the Corinthian church, Paul explained why we are to be generous: "Now he who supplies seed to the sower and bread for food will also supply and increase your store of seed and will enlarge the harvest of your righteousness. You will be *enriched* in every way so that you can be *generous on every occasion*, and through us your generosity will result in thanksgiving to God" (2 Cor. 9:10–11 NIV, emphasis added).

One of the churches I pastored had a very generous member who was a building contractor. This man faithfully tithed his income, which was significant. He also gave above that out of his God-given abundance. One time he handed me a check for twenty thousand dollars. On another occasion he gave sixteen thousand dollars. He knew that a few people would have to know about his contributions, but he asked that the information loop be kept small.

As I expressed my gratitude after he had given one significant gift, the fellow quipped, "It's just part of the deal, right? This is what we are supposed to do." He understood that those to whom God has entrusted much have an obligation to be generous. May his tribe increase, and may his attitude spill over into the local church.

A WILLINGNESS TO RISK

Every worthwhile venture carries risk, and church parenting is no different. Sometimes that risk is a simple willingness to try when failure is a possibility. Has your congregation shown itself willing to take risks? Perhaps it took some risk when it called you as pastor. A church that is willing to ignore the naysayers and try something bold may be a prime candidate for church parenting.

A KINGDOM MIND-SET

Ultimately, parenting churches is not about denominational survival or local church vision. It is about kingdom expansion. A congregation that sees beyond its local or denominational affiliation and recognizes the awesome reach of the kingdom will view church parenting as necessary. The kingdom is expanded very little when a few churches grow larger, but it is greatly increased when churches multiply in a variety of ways.

A pastor friend of mine once told me, "You'll never have to worry about making God mad if you try to plant a church. Whatever ministry you are with, you must understand one thing: Church planting is not for us; it is for God. We do it so God will have a people to worship him." Any church with an eye for the greater harvest field has the potential to become a parenting church.

Any of these indicators create a foundation you can build upon as you prepare your congregation to parent churches. Which of them are already present in your people? Which ones might you cultivate among them?

NEGATIVE INDICATORS

There are times when parenting is not in the best interest of the parent or the potential child. When this is the case, it is better not to rush into parenthood. But how will you know if that is the case? What are the factors that indicate it's not a good time to parent a church?

Here are some caution lights that should raise concern about the timing of a church-parenting effort. Caution lights are not intended to halt forward progress but to raise awareness of potential danger. If your church exhibits any of these yellow lights, it may be better to make parenting a future goal.

MAJOR CHANGE

It is more difficult to complete a parenting project when the parent church is experiencing a major change. Major changes include relocation, an ongoing or just-completed building project, a pastoral transition, or the loss of a large number of members due to conflict, job transfers, or a downturn in the local economy. Changes like these require internal adjustments in the parent church and create less-than-ideal conditions for reproduction.

SPIRITUAL IMMATURITY

It takes an unselfish, mature congregation to parent effectively. If a congregation's spiritual temperature is low, it needs to improve its own health before assuming the responsibility of church parenting. A key indicator of immaturity is an ingrown attitude. A congregation that is always most concerned about itself is immature. Often the result of a self-focused church is infighting over fringe issues, such as the color of carpet for a Sunday school room, the rules for use of the kitchen, the mess the youth group leaves when it uses the fellowship hall, or whether or not to reserve parking spots for visitors and senior adults. All churches address these issues; however, if these matters are the focal point of board meetings, the church is not yet mature and is not in an ideal position to become a parent.

LACK OF LEADERS

In order to successfully parent a church, a congregation needs mature leaders—leaders who are growing forward, not groaning forward. Growing-forward leaders look for ways to stretch their ability and responsibility. Groaning-forward leaders are willing to take steps but not without complaining. Which type of leaders do you have? Are they responsive to the pastor's leadership? Do they engage change easily? Or do they need to develop their understanding of effective leadership?

LACK OF REPRODUCING SYSTEMS

Churches need to have systems that model multiplication if they are to become parents. Sunday school classes and small groups should be trained to reproduce themselves. Leadership training, apprenticeships, and spiritual-gift development programs also aid internal multiplication. Without internal reproduction, a congregation will be hard pressed to invest people in a daughter-church project and then replace those who are invested.

BLURRED FOCUS

An unhealthy church may need to focus on getting healthy before attempting to parent. Refocusing is one tool a church can use to recover its health. Refocusing is a process by which a trained leader helps a congregation refine its sense of identity and purpose.[2] The trained leader helps first the pastor and then key leaders to align themselves with God's unique call on their lives. Ultimately, the church members walk together through steps that empower them for effective ministry. Refocusing moves a church toward health—and healthy churches reproduce.

Does your church exhibit negative indicators for church parenting? Identify them, and form a plan to address them. Above all, remember that the decision to delay church parenting is not the decision to refuse it. Keep church multiplication as a future goal.

TESTING FOR READINESS

When I pastored in Vista, California, a young man served as an intern at our church for one summer. He was from the Midwest and had traveled to California by train. On the day he was to return home, my oldest son and I took him to the train depot. He had quite a bit of luggage, so we helped him stow the bags near his seat. As we were helping him get settled for the long journey, the train suddenly began to move. The conductor pulled up the stairs to shut the door. The train was leaving the station, and neither my son nor I wanted to go with it. I looked at the conductor and said, "I don't want to be on this train."

"Then why are you on this train?" she asked.

I explained that I was there to help a friend with his luggage, but the whole time we were talking, I was thinking, "Weren't you supposed to say 'All aboard!'?"

"Well, you're on the train now," the conductor deadpanned.

"Where is the next stop?" I asked, wondering if we would be traveling all the way to the Midwest.

"San Juan Capistrano," she said, and then she added, "Enjoy the ride."

I considered my situation. San Juan Capistrano is a small community roughly forty-five minutes north of where we lived. Since there was nothing I could do about it, I decided to enjoy the trip and call Joni to come get us in San Juan Capistrano. This changed my plans for the day, but I decided to be flexible.

Unexpected changes are always challenging, and many congregations fear the changes that church parenting will bring. Some simply aren't ready to handle them. At the beginning of any change, you must consider the situation of your church. In this chapter, I have described both positive and negative indicators of a congregation's readiness to parent a church. Evaluate your congregation with these in mind. Consider your present situation, and formulate a plan that will move your congregation toward parenting. As congregational leaders participate in this evaluation, they will gain increased ownership in the vision. Remember, the issue is not *whether* to become involved in church parenting, but *when*.

PART 3

HOW TO PARENT A NEW CHURCH

HOW TO LEAD THE CHARGE 13

The church-parenting ripple begins in the heart of the pastor, but it must spread to the hearts of the pastor's church members. This transfer is not automatic. John Maxwell has said that most pastors' visions do not die at the vision's birth, but in its transition to the congregation. The pastor must communicate the vision for parenting in language that the congregation will understand and accept. The problem, of course, is that adopting that vision will entail change for the church. The congregation will have to accept a change in attitude about the surrounding region, the church facility, the finances, and how ministry is accomplished. And most people don't like change.

UNDERSTANDING CHANGE DYNAMICS

I travel by air regularly, and I admit that I am not a huge fan of in-flight turbulence. I feel most comfortable when the plane is moving forward, not bouncing up and down. I understand some of the factors that create turbulence, but that understanding does not increase my enthusiasm for rough spots. I do appreciate it, though, when the pilot informs the passengers that there will be some turbulence and advises us to fasten our seatbelts. That improves my confidence in the pilot. It also makes it easier to deal with the rough ride.

This "pilot principle" holds true for church life as well. When a leader advises followers to expect change and tells them how to deal with it, the people's confidence level goes up, and they are more willing to make the journey. Note that the pilot never apologizes for the turbulence—only for the inconvenience it may cause. The turbulence of change is unavoidable, but a leader can lessen the inconvenience it brings through foresight, preparation, and communication.

Some leaders seem unaware of the effects of change on their followers. That may be because leaders usually love change. After all, they initiate it! So if you have embraced the idea of church parenting, you are probably raring to get started. You have already weighed the pros and cons. You are convinced that your church should use this method of evangelism, and you're ready to begin the adventure. But the members of your congregation are in a different position. They have just been introduced to the idea of church parenting and have not had time to process it adequately. You can expect them to be resistant.

Resistance is the initial response of people to any change. Congregational resistance to church parenting may come as a vague feeling that says, "I'm not sure I like this." Or it may be seen in an entrenched attitude accompanied by the tune to "We Shall Not Be Moved." But initial resistance is not the same as rejection or defiance. It is simply part of the natural process of accepting change.

Leaders are often frustrated by resistance, because they expect an open-armed welcome for their new ideas. Initial resistance sometimes catches leaders the way a deer is caught in the headlights—they're puzzled and unsure about what to do next. "What is wrong with these people?" a leader may wonder. "Why don't they want to be led? If they were godly, they would get on board with this."

One reason people resist church parenting is that they do not understand what it entails. Their initial resistance is a call for more information. It provides the pastor an opportunity to lead by anticipating and answering questions such as the following:

- What does it mean to parent a church?
- What impact will this have on us?
- When would we do this?
- How much will it cost?
- Do I have to go to the daughter church?
- Why do we have to get involved in this?
- Pastor, does this mean you are leaving?

The bottom line is that people want to know how a proposed change might affect them and how it will be accomplished.

When my kids were younger, they often approached me after a worship service and asked permission to do something. At what seemed to them an opportune moment, they would ask,

"May we go to so-and-so's house?" Usually, I had several questions about the request but couldn't ask them because I was in the middle of a conversation with a parishioner. "Wait a few minutes," was my usual reply. Like most kids, however, mine were a little impatient and would press for a decision. Finally, I would say, "If you want my decision now, then the answer is no. But if you wait until I can think about it for a minute, the answer might be different." They were always willing to wait.

Was I resistant to their requests? Often, I was. Did that mean I rejected the idea? No, I simply had questions that needed to be answered before I could make a positive decision. When church leaders rush in with a plan and ask for an immediate decision, the congregation will resist—no matter how good the idea is. The more pressure leaders apply, the more resistance they will meet.

When you present the idea of church parenting to your people, be prepared for the turbulence it will bring. Understand the congregation's need for information, and provide it. Come with ready answers to as many questions as possible. Help people see the journey ahead, and equip them to prepare for the changes it will bring. And be patient. It will take time for the church-parenting ripple to spread from your heart to theirs.

MANAGING CHANGE EFFECTIVELY

Leading a major change like church parenting seems like a daunting task, but it is something that nearly every leader can accomplish by paying attention to some basics. Providing information will help a congregation embrace the idea of church planting and move toward a new course of action. From there, the following seven simple steps will minimize the turbulence of change and lead to a successful church-multiplication effort. Remember this basic plan with the acronym CHANGES.

C—CAST A VISION

To lead a church-parenting effort, you must be a vision-caster. Casting the vision for church multiplication enables people to adopt goals that are outside their own perceived interests. Church planting involves reaching people that the parent-church congregation may never see. Vision casting takes creativity, because it involves rallying people to an intangible goal. It is one thing to help people see a building that is not yet built; it is quite another to help them envision a body of believers that doesn't currently exist.

The dot-com revolution brought to the forefront the idea that a business does not have to be composed of brick and mortar. You can move away from brick-and-mortar vision casting by opening the congregation's eyes to people and places rather than to walls and roofs. Does this imply that owning property and constructing buildings are somehow contrary to church parenting? No, but moving a congregation to create a daughter church requires a different approach than moving people to embark on a building project.

H—HAVE AN END IN MIND

In 1990 I led a mission team to Munich, Germany. While we were there, an unexpected ministry opportunity presented itself when our team was invited to visit a Christian youth camp near Budapest, Hungary. We accepted the offer, loaded up two vans, and headed for the Hungarian countryside. We traveled late into the night. It was close to midnight and very dark, and I was following the lead van driven by the host missionary. It appeared to me that we were wandering aimlessly through the darkened landscape, but I assumed the missionary knew where he was going.

Suddenly, the lead van pulled to the side of the road. I quickly followed suit. The missionary jumped out of his van and ran back toward the vehicle I was driving. I jumped out to meet him halfway. I was concerned. Was there a problem?

"We are looking for a buffa," the missionary informed me. "We need to turn left at the buffa."

"What's a buffa?" I asked.

Without cracking a smile, the missionary said, "I don't know." With that he turned and ran back toward his van. Amazingly, we found the buffa—a small store—and arrived at our destination.

When you begin the church-parenting journey, your congregation may feel that you are wandering aimlessly. It will put your people at ease if you can clearly describe your destination—the daughter church. Tell them what it will look like. Describe what a parent church should look like. Provide a biblical framework for parenting. Talk about the joys and privileges of parenting a congregation. As you point toward a clear destination, others will begin to see the value of a regional ministry. Their enthusiasm will be heightened as they catch sight of the ripples from their church reaching some distant shore.

A—ADVANCE STRATEGICALLY

I admire people who play chess well. It is incredible to me how they advance the pieces strategically, often planning several moves in advance. Yet when an opponent makes some unexpected move, a good player will adjust his or her planned response. A skilled chess player can envision the endgame well in advance and plan a strategy to achieve it.

Advancing toward the goal of church parenting requires strategic planning. To create a daughter congregation, your church will need a parent action plan, a comprehensive blueprint for your project.[1] No action plan may be set in stone, however. Be willing to change the plan as needed. John Maxwell, in his wonderful little book *People Power: Life's Little Lessons on Relationships*, shares the following nugget he garnered from his friend Jim Dornan: "Write the goal in concrete and the plan in sand."[2] The goal is to parent a growing, healthy, reproducing church—never compromise on that. But the plan may have to be changed, just as a chess player has to adjust his or her strategy during a match.

Bill Dave has been a mentor of mine for years. He retired after thirty-five years as the civilian administrator of a large air force base in Sacramento. Bill knows what it takes to get a diverse group of people to rally around a common cause. At one of our mentoring appointments, Bill gave me this advice: "Phil, don't ever sanctify deadlines." As parent-church leaders, we can easily get caught up in deadlines. When we have declared that we will parent a church by a certain date, it becomes tempting to force the result. But the deadline is not what matters—the creation of a new, healthy, reproducing church is. If achieving that result means changing a deadline, do it. Allow the Spirit of God, not the plan, to dictate the timing.

N—NEGOTIATE THE PROBLEMS

As the church-parenting ripple expands through your congregation, problems will arise. Anticipate them; don't ignore them.

The better you anticipate problems, the better you will handle them. Here are some common challenges.

Ignorance. Some problems arise from a congregation's ignorance of church parenting. At the beginning, they know little about the process. They have not had time to consider the idea fully. That brings resistance. The solution to ignorance is information. Provide it. Overcome the problem of ignorance by anticipating questions and answering them.

Apathy. People tend to be disinterested in those with whom they have little in common. Many church members can see little reason to reach beyond their immediate community. The solution to apathy is allegiance to the gospel message. Overcome apathy by elevating the evangelistic mission of the church.

Arrogance. A congregation that has what it needs may see no reason to help others get what they need. "We worked for our resources!" some will say. "Let new churches work for their own." The solution to arrogance is brokenness. Pray for personal and corporate brokenness over the lost. If there is not genuine brokenness in your church for unsaved people, ask God to provide it.

Distrust. It takes trust in God to parent a new congregation. Often it is easier for a believer to trust God individually than for a congregation to trust him corporately. The solution to lack of trust is willing faith. Hold the promises of God before your people along with the challenge to accept them. Take God at his word.

G—GET THE CONGREGATION ONBOARD

When I served on the pastoral staff of Dr. John Maxwell, he would often say, "He who thinks he is leading but has no one following is simply taking a walk." A pastor's enthusiasm for church parenting will mean nothing if the congregation does not follow.

Many leaders believe they can enact their vision for church multiplication through a strong will and persistent effort—and some can. But it is a mistake to move ahead without ensuring that the congregation has ownership of the result. You want people on the ship with you, not waving good-bye to you from the pier. How might you accomplish that?

Work inside out. Begin with your leadership team, which might be your church board or ministry team. When these leaders catch the church-parenting vision, they will help it infiltrate the congregation. Put resources into your leaders' hands. Take them to seminars on church multiplication. Share your vision with them one-on-one.

Also communicate your vision through preaching and teaching. Preach on the biblical value of church parenting. Teach a topical series from the book of Acts. Show how the early church expanded through multiplication. Show your people that the gospel is spread through believers winning the lost to Christ and starting new churches.

Be careful to provide information in bite-sized pieces. Remember the old gag, "How do you eat an elephant? One bite at a time." It would be unwise to stand before the congregation and declare that your church will begin parenting in six months. That would be like offering them a drink of water from a fire hose. Share the vision over an extended period of time.

It may help to invite church-planting leaders to give their testimonies. Invite not only planting pastors but also laypeople who have helped begin another church. Such testimonies will open the eyes of your people to opportunities they never knew existed.

E—EVALUATE PROGRESS

In the top left corner of my car's windshield, there is a sticker containing several numbers. The numbers represent projected mileage. When my odometer matches those numbers, I'll know it is time to have the car's oil changed and its fluids checked. This regular checkup is critical for the efficient operation of my car.

Checkups are also important for managing the process of change in a church. Schedule regular evaluation times for determining whether or not the plan is moving on schedule. Keep the desired result in mind, but be willing to change specific steps as necessary to keep the process going smoothly.

S—SHOW THE RESULTS

Results provide motivation. Parenting congregations must see a return on their investment, or they will lose enthusiasm for church multiplication. Once the new church plant is underway, provide information to the parent congregation about the daughter church—conversions, baptisms, and attendance. Invite new people from the daughter church to share the impact of Christ upon their lives. The parent church needs to see the influence it has had for God through the new congregation.

Through one of the daughter churches I've been involved with, a man renewed his relationship with Christ and began attending church again. This fellow was invited to share his testimony at the parent church one Sunday morning, and he became a living example of the unseen impact of the parent congregation. After the service one of our members approached me and said, "Thanks for reminding me of why we do this." The results were clear.

GAINING AGREEMENT

Scripture teaches that without a vision, the people perish (see Prov. 29:18). At one conference I attended, Sean Randall, a church planter in Sparks, Nevada, put an interesting twist on that verse. He said, "Without a people, the vision will perish." That is especially true of church parenting. A leader may begin the ripple, but unless the people participate, the ripple will never reach the shore. One leader's vision is never enough to sustain a church multiplication movement.

As a ripple leader, you must cast the vision for church parenting among your people. There will be resistance, for no change of this magnitude is easily accepted. Remember the pilot principle: When a leader advises followers to expect change and tells them how to deal with it, the people's confidence level goes up, and they are more willing to make the journey. You are the key to managing change in your congregation. Anticipate it, prepare for it, and communicate it. Don't allow the vision to perish.

14 HOW TO FINANCE A PARENTED CHURCH

Making kingdom waves is not without monetary cost. Parent congregations must make a significant financial investment in planting a new church. The funds, in most cases, must be intentionally set aside for the purpose. Yet present planning leads to the realization of future goals. Every church can finance its own multiplication through discipline, planning, and partnership.

MORE WITH LESS

The Old Testament prophet Elisha worked many miracles. One of his greatest exploits involved an encounter with a poor widow. This often-cited story holds a great lesson for congregations that want to expand the kingdom through church multiplication. It is found in 2 Kings 4:1–7.

One day a widow came to Elisha. Her husband had been a prophet along with Elisha, and his death had left the woman in a difficult situation. The family owed some debts, and if the widow was unable to pay them, she would lose her sons to slavery. The widow had no financial resources to meet the need; she was desperate.

"What do you have in the house?" (4:2) Elisha queried, a rather odd question to ask a destitute woman. Yet Elisha was concerned with what the woman had available to her, not with what she needed. The widow's first response is typical of anyone facing an overwhelming financial challenge: "Nothing at all" (4:2). If she'd had any resources, she wouldn't be facing this crisis, right? But then something clicked in her mind. No sooner had those words escaped her mouth than she remembered something that she did have—a little oil. It may have been a small amount, but it was enough to meet her need, as Elisha soon showed her.

Established churches that contemplate church parenting often feel the same way the widow initially did. It costs a great deal to finance a church start, and prospective parent churches usually say, "We can't afford it." Church leaders review their budgets and conclude that they don't have the financial resources to parent a congregation. Yet they neglect to consider the value of what little they do have.

Elisha instructed the widow to collect empty jars from her neighbors and then fill them with oil from her one small jar. Miraculously, the woman's little bit of oil filled every spare jar in town, and the widow was able to sell the oil to raise money and pay her debts. A congregation's resources may seem scanty, but God can use them to help fund church parenting. Churches do not need an existing surplus in order to parent. With proper planning—and faith—even small resources can fund a church plant.

THE BEST TIME TO BEGIN

The best time to plant a tree was twenty years ago; the next best time is now. When making financial plans for church parenting, it does no good to bemoan the fact that you didn't start earlier. It is far better to begin simply. Financial planners know this simple formula: consistent investment plus extended time equals increased resources. The amount you invest need not be large, but you must set it aside consistently. Time is the investor's ally. If your congregation has not yet begun to set money aside for church parenting, now is the time.

When I got married twenty-eight years ago, an older man pulled me aside and said, "Phil, if you wait to have children until you can afford it, you never will." At the time his words made little sense to me. Starting a family was the furthest thing from my mind. Joni and I had been married only a month or so. I just wanted to be a husband, not a dad. As I look back, however, the advice made perfect sense. If we had waited until we had all the money we might need before having children, we probably still wouldn't be parents. We made the best financial preparations we could—including having health insurance—but we did not wait for the "perfect time" to have kids. If your congregation waits until it can afford to parent a new church, it probably never will. It is true that your church will need a financial plan, one that includes the key coverage you'll need to become a parent. But the "perfect time" to become a parent church will never arrive.

FUNDING FROM THE PARENT CHURCH

Basketball coach Bobby Knight is credited with saying, "The will to prepare is more important than the will to win." After one of his many political defeats, Abraham Lincoln told a colleague, "I will prepare, and my time will come." Jesus said, "Suppose one of you wants to build a tower. Won't you first sit down and estimate the cost to see if you have enough money to complete it?" (Luke 14:28 NIV). The bottom line is this: You must prepare financially if you want to multiply successfully.

A parent church typically provides some financial support to its daughter. Just as married couples sometimes begin college funds for their children even before they are born, parent churches must plan ahead to meet the financial needs of their children. Here are six ways to begin making financial preparations for the birth of a daughter congregation. They are not painless, but they are not overly painful. Any church with the will to multiply can finance the effort—with a little discipline.

TEACH GENEROSITY

Teach generosity to your congregation. Encourage your people to give beyond themselves. A generous church knows how to sacrifice. That church also knows the joy that comes from sharing with others. One practical way to teach generosity is to provide opportunities to give away money. Arcade Wesleyan Church began collecting an annual offering at its Christmas Eve service. This offering was given to one new church each year. The offering was announced well ahead of the service, but there was no goal amount; it was a simple freewill offering. This practice kept the goal of church parenting before the congregation, and it taught the people how to share with others.

You might develop an offering associated with a special day and have some fun with it. One church designated Super Bowl Sunday as a special offering day. Each person was asked to bring a roll of quarters—ten dollars. Goal posts were constructed from PVC pipe, and with football-themed music playing, people threw their quarter rolls through the uprights and into a collection basket.

PRACTICE THE 10 PERCENT RULE

Many churches have surplus funds at the end of the year. In other words, they did not spend every dollar they collected. Try taking 10 percent of your church's surplus and putting it into a church-planting fund. You will be amazed at the amount of money that will accrue in just a few years.

The River Church in Sacramento, California, has taken this concept to a new level. From its birth, the leaders determined to give away 10 percent of the church's income. Even after a number of years, each month the people of River Church still invest 10 percent of their tithes and offerings outside themselves. They give to overseas missions, make gifts to the school from which they rent facilities, or support other worthwhile projects. They have even given this money to congregation members and asked them to use it to bless someone outside the church. One of these monthly gifts each year is set aside for the support of their future daughter church.

HOST A BABY SHOWER

A parent church can support a daughter church financially by sponsoring a "baby shower" for the new congregation. As with any shower, the host lists items that the new baby will need. In the case of a baby church, those would be items needed to conduct worship services, equip an office, or supply Christian education classes. Members of the parent church bring gifts to a shower, complete with cake and punch, and present them to the church planter and core team members. Wrapping the gifts can make the shower even more fun.

MAKE PARENTING A BUDGET ITEM

Include church planting as a line item in your church's annual budget. Treat church-planting expenses like a bill, and pay them monthly. Be as tenacious in setting aside money for this purpose as you are about paying the church's mortgage or utility bills. You could choose to make church planting part of your church's missions budget. Churches often separate domestic and foreign missions in their thinking, but both are part of the same world-mission effort. Shouldn't we desire to reach those in our own communities just as much as we want to reach those around the world?

One church of about eighty people got involved in parenting by giving each year to a new church. They put church planting into their missions budget and set aside one hundred dollars per month. The pastor dreams of seeing this congregation parent a church someday. When the time comes, a financial commitment to the project will have already been built into the church's financial structure.

INVEST IN OTHERS

Be willing to invest in others while you invest in yourself. One pastor wanted to incorporate preparation for church parenting into everything his congregation did. When the church needed to raise funds for a new sanctuary, it made a commitment to place 10 percent of the money received into its church parenting fund.

ESTABLISH A MEMORIAL FUND

We often see memorial funds used to finance building projects. Why not use gifts in memory or in honor of loved ones to support church parenting? When people inquire about designating memorial gifts, suggest church parenting. What better memorial could there be for a believer than a new, living church?

These few examples should do little more than get you started in devising ways to support church parenting. Creative leaders will think of dozens more. The secret is to begin preparing now, even with a small amount. A little, invested over time, will result in an abundance of resources. But you must begin. Financial preparation is a matter of the will more than of anything else.

FUNDING FROM THE DAUGHTER CHURCH

My son Scott was preparing to purchase a vehicle. As he was putting money aside, he drove one of our cars. We made the payments on the car, but he was responsible for all other expenses associated with it. He paid for the insurance. He bought his own gas. He covered the cost of oil changes and other maintenance. This arrangement enabled him to begin driving immediately, and it also made him a financial partner in the effort. Being financially responsible helped Scott appreciate the value of the car he was driving.

Daughter churches need to be financial partners in their own startup. If the parent church pays for everything, the daughter may fail to appreciate the cost of its existence. Starting a church works best as a cooperative venture between the new congregation, the parent church, and the denomination or association, since all three entities have a vested interest in the outcome of the project. Here are some creative ways to involve daughter churches in their own financial health.

GET A FINANCIAL COMMITMENT FROM THE CORE GROUP

The members of your daughter church's core group will be mature Christians. It's likely that they will be people who tithe their income to your church. When they join the core team, they should be asked to transfer their financial commitment to the daughter church. This core group will provide a nucleus of financial support for the church plant, and that's vital. Every daughter church must be partly responsible for its own support.

CREATE A BOOMERANG MENTALITY

When parenting a congregation, create the expectation in the daughter church that it will someday be responsible to invest back into the parent. Many parent churches ask each of the daughter churches to reinvest a certain amount of money back into the parent church for future multiplication efforts. This "family" money is paid to the parent church within the first two years and is later used to plant more churches. This approach builds a spirit of generosity and partnership into the culture of the new church.

HAVE THE CHURCH PLANTER RAISE SUPPORT

In every church plant, the church planter, or start-up pastor, must raise some funds personally. This creates a sense of ownership in the project for him or her and wards off a potential welfare mentality, which expects support by every means except one's own effort.[1]

REQUIRE THE PASTOR TO BE BIVOCATIONAL

Often new churches do not have the income to pay their pastor a full-time salary. In such cases, the planter should be willing to seek employment outside the church. Having a bivocational pastor may seem like a drawback, but it offers some advantages to a new congregation. It causes the planter to have a greater personal interest in church finances. Also, a bivocational pastor will support the church by tithing on his outside income. And working in the community keeps the planter connected to the unchurched. Work relationships can yield insights into community concerns and provide witnessing opportunities.

Michael Barnett relocated his family from Minneapolis to San Diego to plant a church in the summer of 2011. He knew he would need employment to help with his support. He chose to get a job in solar panel sales. He wanted a high-risk, high-reward position. He also wanted to be in a place where he could connect with those who are disconnected from Christ. He has found both.

A daughter church should pay something toward the salary of its pastor, and bivocational employment is not the church planter's long-term goal. Establishing an early habit of conducting budget and salary reviews will help the leadership team make a timely transition to providing full-time support for the church planter.

SEEK A PASTOR WITH ALTERNATIVE SOURCES OF INCOME

Some church planters can subsidize their ministry through further sources of income, one example being the support of a working spouse. When a pastor's spouse works outside the home, his or her income can free the planter to focus on starting the church. It also provides the planter a connection to the unchurched community.

In Nampa, Idaho, the wife of a church planter worked as a fitness instructor in a local health club. She met many young mothers, and the relationships she built with them provided an open door for her to invite them to church. Dozens of families came to the church as a result of this inroad.

ASK FOR DENOMINATIONAL FUNDING

It is the role of denominations to create an environment for church parenting, and that includes funding. The idea, however, is that the denomination should provide supplemental funding. The denomination should not be the sole supporter of a church plant. Here are three types of denominational funding that may be used to supplement a parenting effort.

Matching Funds. Church parenting can be encouraged when a denomination provides matching funds to parent churches. The denomination informs the parent church that a certain amount is available on a matching basis. The amount should be limited. That is, the denomination agrees to match funds up to a designated amount.

Value-Added Funds. A denomination may choose to invest in a parenting effort by underscoring key values. For example, the denomination might pay for planter coaching or parent-church training because it believes that these functions are essential. Or a denomination might provide health insurance or a housing allowance for the planting team to underscore the value of adequately supporting the team.

Budget Breaks. Most denominations have some system of collecting funds from their churches. This money is used to support the organization and its ministries. Generally, the assessment is not voluntary; the churches are assessed a certain annual sum based on established criteria. Denominations can provide a "break" for parent churches by temporarily reducing their financial obligation to the denomination. That not only benefits the church plant, but also speeds the recovery of the parent church.

Parenting healthy reproducing churches is a team effort. Denominational structures can contribute much to create a vibrant multiplication environment.

THE PAYOFF

Is there a financial cost to ripple making? Absolutely, but it is a reasonable cost. Through planning, persistence, and partnering with others, financing a parenting project is a reachable goal for every congregation. Now is the time to begin. Don't wait until you can afford to parent, or you may never do it. When you're tempted to think, "We can't afford to parent a church," remember instead that you can't afford not to.

And think of the rewards. Investments, of course, are made with the hope of a return. The return of church parenting funds is not dollars and cents. The return is a multiplication of the kingdom. The dollars we invest do not merely buy brick and mortar. They establish new, healthy, reproducing churches—churches that will add souls to the kingdom for years to come. Isn't that an investment worth making?

15 HOW TO BUILD A PARENTING TEAM

It had been one of those long days that pastors sometimes experience. I had gone to the church early that morning, and I'd had appointments into the evening. I had led a Bible study that night, which meant that I hadn't gone home for dinner.

Finally, after our evening programs were concluded, I waved good-bye to the technicians who were tinkering with the sound system and headed for home. I was looking forward to putting my feet up and having a Pepsi and a bowl of popcorn as Joni and I watched one of our favorite television programs.

When I entered the house, Joni asked, "Where's Megan?" Megan, our daughter, was eleven years old at the time.

"I don't know," I said. "I thought she was with you." The look on Joni's face told me that I thought wrong.

"I left her at church," she said. "She was going to come home with you." The tone of my lovely wife's voice let me know there would be no discussion as to who would go back and get Megan. Joni and I had both made an assumption. Each of us thought the other would be responsible for looking after our daughter. As a result, no one took responsibility until there was a problem.

The same thing can happen in parent churches. The pastor and the laity may both assume that someone else is responsible for leading the parenting effort. Laypeople may think the pastor will head up the project, while the pastor believes it's the congregation's responsibility to do the job. As a result, the parenting process never begins or, worse yet, stalls soon after starting. The ripple will never reach the water's edge unless pastors and laypersons take mutual responsibility for church parenting. It takes a team to plant a church.

During my senior year in high school, I played on a football team that won its league championship. That achievement would have seemed farfetched during my first two years of high-school competition. During those two years, our team's record was 0-1-17. That's zero wins, one tie, and seventeen losses! The tie occurred in the first game I played in high school. Little did I know that it would be the highlight of my first two seasons.

During my junior year, though, everything changed. Players started practicing harder. We gained skill. We began to play better, and we began to win. By the end of my senior year, we had become champions. What happened? We had gotten a new head coach, Dwight Morris; he made all the difference. Coach Morris knew that the secret to success in football is to form a group of individuals into a team. And he understood the components needed to build a winning team: the right players, good preparation, a purpose, and a plan. When the right people come together for the right purpose, anything is possible.

That's why churches are planted most effectively by purpose-driven teams. Ministry teams always trump committees. The very word *committee* conjures up the image of a slow-moving, visionless, and stodgy group of people. This is a bit overstated, perhaps, but committees seldom inspire progress and innovation. Committees are focused on process. The word *team*, on the other hand, implies action and purpose. Teams are focused on a goal, and they discover methods to reach that goal.

It's vital to assemble a team for creating a reproducing church. A parenting team is brought together for a purpose, then disbanded when the mission is accomplished. If a church parents regularly, a new team can be assembled for each new plant. Doing this will involve more people in the process, and the more people who are involved, the greater the sense of ownership within the congregation will be. Here are the steps to building a winning church-parenting team.

DETERMINE THE COMPOSITION OF THE TEAM

Coach Morris inherited a group of players, but he wasn't obligated to use that group. He knew the kind of players he was looking for: guys who would be willing to sacrifice for the team. He wanted individuals who would build up one another, not tear down one other. One of his first tasks was to select players who had the right attitude.

When putting together a team that will take the ripple to the water's edge, look for players who have the right stuff. You want a team that is well-led and displays the right characteristics.

MEMBER CHARACTERISTICS

Teamwork. Team members must affirm the value of teamwork over individual accomplishment. They must be willing to work together. If they view themselves as a collection of individuals instead of a unified core, there will be conflict.

Commitment. Team members must be sold on the idea of church parenting and fully committed to it. Placing people on the team will not convince them of the need to parent. You want only those who are already convinced of this calling to serve there.

Evangelistic Zeal. To serve effectively on a parenting team, members must believe in evangelism. They must further believe that church planting is the most effective method of evangelism. Evangelistic thinkers will have a passion to build the kingdom by planting new churches.

Optimism. Parenting is a challenging endeavor, so you do not want naysayers on your team. Recruit people who can find the opportunity in every obstacle.

Faith. Team members must be people of faith. They must be willing to believe God for the impossible. Parenting team members must embrace a vision of what a parenting congregation looks like. They must be able to look beyond what is seen into the unseen. That takes faith.

MEMBER GIFTS

In addition to these characteristics, which you will want in every person on the team, you'll want to see specific gifts displayed by various members.

Strategic Thinking. You will need at least one strategic thinker, someone who is adept at reasoning through a process. This person understands goals, objectives, plans, and strategic steps. Strategic thinkers typically ask penetrating questions.

Institutional Memory. A church historian makes a helpful team member. He or she knows the personality and dynamics of your congregation and can give you a sense of where it has been spiritually and emotionally. A historian helps the team avoid repeating mistakes. A long-tenured pastor is likely such a person.

Ministry Involvement. People who are active in the church's ministry will contribute greatly to the team's effectiveness. You do not need to have every Sunday school class, interest group, or ministry represented. This would make a cumbersome team. Determine which groups are most critical to the success of the parenting effort and involve them.

Creative Thinking. Creative thinkers are an asset to a parenting team. Church parenting is not a conservative endeavor. You want people who see things a bit off-center. These people will stretch the team, forcing others to break free from the confines of conventional wisdom. Often, free thinkers will irritate others with their unique way of viewing the parenting process. That creative tension will force the team to consider new options and to think clearly about the choices it makes.

TEAM LEADERSHIP

I am frequently asked, "Who should lead the team?" The team leader should be a significant member of the parent church's pastoral staff, ideally the senior pastor. If he or she is unable to function in this role, a highly regarded staff member should lead. The status of the team leader communicates the importance of parenting to the congregation.

TEAM SIZE

How many members should serve on a church parenting team? This is left to the discretion of the pastoral leaders. Guard against the team becoming too cumbersome and unmanageable. A lean team is an effective team.

Patrick Lencioni, in his book *The Advantage*, talks about what makes a leadership team effective. He suggests that the team should be on the smaller side. He contends that the smaller the team, the more effective it is: "The leadership team [should be] small enough (three to ten people) to be effective."[1] I think this is an excellent guideline.

CAREFULLY RECRUIT TEAM MEMBERS

When you have an idea of the desired composition of the team, you can begin recruiting. Team selection begins with prayer. Before you recruit your parenting team, recruit a small intercessory team to support it. The intercessors' role is to pray for the team members, for openness in the hearts of congregation members, for the church planter, and for the spiritual preparation of potential planting locations. Prayer is the backbone of the parenting process.

Next develop a ministry description for parent team members. This description should include key expectations, responsibilities, and time commitments required.

Then ask key church leaders to suggest potential parent team members. Poll board members, small-group leaders, Sunday school teachers, and other leaders. Share the team's ministry description with them, and ask them to suggest people who would be a good fit. Prayerfully pare down the list to a manageable number. Remove from consideration anyone who does not meet the team criteria. When you have reduced the list to two or three names more than your goal number of participants, you're ready to recruit.

The next step is to meet individually with potential members. Meeting face-to-face for coffee or a meal with your prospective teammates emphasizes to them the importance of the parenting project. When you meet, share the team's vision and ministry description with them, and review your expectations for each person who will serve on this team. Allow opportunity to ask questions. Do not press potential team members for their commitment at the conclusion of this meeting; you do not want a premature response, whether yes or no. Candidates need time, probably a week, to prayerfully consider their involvement. Follow up the meeting with a phone call—don't ask them to call you.

Coach Morris knew that if his players were in good physical condition, they could begin working sooner on offensive and defensive plans. And the better you lay the groundwork for your team, the sooner the team can begin the actual work of planning the parenting project.

Once the team is in place, call its first meeting within two weeks. The sooner you begin planning, the sooner the dream of parenting will come to fruition.

OUTLINE THE TEAM'S PURPOSE

I can still remember our first team meeting with my high-school football coach, Dwight Morris. He told us that our purpose was twofold: work hard and win a championship. He summed up things with these words: "The team that wins in this league is the team that works the hardest. No team will work harder than we will." If nothing else, we knew what lay ahead of us that year; we knew our purpose.

The parenting team's purpose is simple: develop a plan for the effective parenting of a healthy, reproducing church. Its purpose is not to make a plan for the actual planting of the church; the planter is responsible for those details. The parenting team is to devise a plan that will put in place the elements needed to parent a church.

Parent-church teams often get caught up in the wrong aspect of planning. They think it is their responsibility to determine the location, the target audience, and the steps needed to start the church. That isn't their job. The parenting team is responsible to prepare the parent congregation for church planting. The team leader must clearly identify that purpose for the team and then keep it working toward that goal. The parenting team will be responsible for at least the following actions:

- To identify and recruit intercessors who will pray for the parenting project;
- To communicate to the congregation a biblical understanding of parenting;
- To develop for the church a biblical understanding of the directive to parent;
- To create awareness among the congregation of the process of change that awaits the church;
- To clarify relationships with and mutual expectations of denominational leaders and the planting pastor; and

- To create a timeline for the project and to identify critical milestones for the church to reach along the way.

Teams are a necessary component of developing and implementing a parent action plan. Building the team correctly, giving it the right tools, and clarifying your expectations of it strengthens this team. When you have the right team that has the right tools and shares the same goal, you have created a sharp-edged instrument for effectiveness.

HOW TO BUILD A PARENT ACTION PLAN

16

Seldom do churches just spring into existence. Healthy churches result from proper planning and implementation. Your team will need to crystallize its dream into a clear action plan. When I was in high school, Coach Morris devised offensive and defensive plans for our team. Coach approached this task with an interesting philosophy. Instead of presenting a preselected offensive strategy and trying to make the players implement it, he evaluated the talent of the team and then designed his offensive strategy accordingly. The plays we used were designed to fit the players, not vice versa.

That is exactly the way a church-parenting team should devise its action plan. Begin by evaluating the congregation; each one is different. A plan that works for one may not be suitable for another. A workable parenting plan ought to include five key actions.

CHOOSE A MODEL

First, determine the parenting model that you will use. Review the intentional parenting models listed in chapter 9. In light of your congregation's strengths, abilities, and attitudes, which model will work best for you?

SET EXPECTATIONS

Second, set expectations for the parenting project. We all have expectations about our involvement in any given endeavor and the results it will bring. Incorrectly communicating or not communicating those expectations can result in frustration and misunderstanding.

I once coached a church planter in western Canada. During our first meeting, I discovered that he was frustrated by uneasiness between him and the officials of his denomination. As we discussed the matter, it became clear that neither party had laid down clear expectations. The planter believed that he was right on track, planting a wonderful church. Yet the denomination's leaders believed the project—and their investment—had gone awry. Each party was working from a different set of expectations. The parenting team can avoid this trap by devising clear expectations and communicating them to the parent congregation, the daughter church, and the denomination.

EXPECTATIONS FOR THE PARENT CHURCH

When determining expectations, consider the following questions: What can the daughter church expect from the parent?

What resources will be made available to it? How long will the parent invest in the daughter?

A key principle is that the parent should underpromise and overdeliver. For example, if the parent church promises five thousand dollars in support but is able to invest ten thousand, the daughter congregation will be overjoyed. Now reverse that situation. If the parent church promises ten thousand dollars but is able to provide only five thousand, the daughter church may feel betrayed.

The daughter church should expect that support will not be cut off immediately after its birth. Parent congregations sometimes cut off their new church financially, emotionally, or organizationally too soon. An infant congregation may not survive alone. An effective parenting plan will allow adequate time for the new church to stabilize. The amount of time needed will vary depending on the size of the core team and the upfront financial investment of the parent. The parent congregation should clarify the length of time that the daughter can count on receiving support from it. However, it may be necessary to be flexible in light of the current situation when that deadline arrives.

On the other hand, the parent should avoid becoming an overbearing presence in the life of its child. There are times when a parent church will not allow the new church to grow. Layers of expectation are placed on the daughter, which result in keeping the new church dependent on the parent for too long. The action plan must foresee cutting the apron strings and letting the daughter church become responsible for herself.

EXPECTATIONS FOR OTHERS

There will be expectations, stated or unstated, for other parties that are involved in the church planting effort. The daughter church, the planting pastor, and the parenting pastor will each have responsibilities. It is best to clarify them at the beginning of the project and then communicate them to everyone involved.

What can the parent expect from the daughter? When will the daughter be self-sufficient? What communication should come from the daughter? What kind of reporting is expected from this church, and how frequently should it be made?

What is expected of the parent-church pastor? He or she must give people permission to go with the planter. No one but the senior pastor can do this. The parent-church pastor must also provide the planter with some exposure to the parent congregation and allow him or her to recruit core team members. That exposure might take the form of preaching opportunities, teaching Sunday school classes, or anything that will cast the planter in a positive light.

What is expected of the daughter-church pastor? One of the biggest errors in church planting is having the right place but the wrong planter. As the parenting team selects a planter, it must seek an individual who will fit into the potential planting community and who shares the philosophy of church multiplication. When parenting congregations, I was never interested in working with a planter who wanted to plant only one church. We were starting a multiplication movement, not planting a solitary church; therefore, we looked for planters who wanted to plant reproducing churches and become parent pastors themselves someday.

Also, the planter must be loyal to the parent-church pastor. The planter should not possess a sense of competitiveness or one-upmanship toward the parent pastor. And the planter is responsible to grant permission for people to remain at the parent church. He or she must not make people feel like second-class believers because they do not sense a call to the church plant. The planter must present the new church as an extension of the vision of the parent church. The new church must not be seen as a means of finally "doing church right."

ARRANGE FINANCING

Third, determine a plan for financing the church plant. There are many ways to underwrite the planting of a new church. Review the ideas for financing a church-parenting effort in chapter 9, and determine which method or methods best suit your situation.

ESTABLISH RECRUITING METHODS

Fourth, the action plan must address the manner in which core team members from the parent church will be recruited to become part of the daughter church. Without careful communication to the congregation, recruitment can be a quagmire. The parenting team must establish guidelines that allow a planter to recruit members from the parent congregation. In the parenting endeavors I have led, we gave our planters two instructions: (1) Anyone may be recruited except for staff members; and (2) recruiting must be done only within a designated five-month timeframe. These guidelines worked well for us. You will need to develop guidelines that work for you and your congregation.

PLAN FOR RECOVERY

Finally, the parenting team must include an action plan for recovering from the parenting effort. My biggest mistake in parenting, by far, was not giving the parent church enough time to recover. I underestimated the impact the birth of a new church would have on the parent congregation, and I underestimated the impact it would have on me. Just as many new moms experience postpartum blues, many parent churches experience post-planting blues. These blues are the sense of loss felt by the parent congregation and pastor. The parenting team should prepare for this and make a plan to deal with it. The parent church needs some R & R—recovery and rejuvenation—after giving birth. Expect it, and plan for it.

Developing an action plan may not come naturally to the parenting team members. It is wise to arrange for some training on how to develop a plan. Consider enlisting a coach to help the parent church team through this process. Someone who has successfully led his or her congregation through a parenting process would be an ideal coach. And remember that the plan must not be stagnant; it must be flexible to meet changing circumstances within the congregation.[1]

At the back of this book you will find a resource you can use to work with your leadership team to develop a first-draft parent action plan. It is designed around a one-day retreat. Following these steps will guide you and your team down the path to becoming a ripple church.

BE A MOVEMENT MAKER

Church-planting movements happen when churches and church leaders are committed to the exponential growth of God's kingdom. David Garrison, in his book *Church Planting Movements*, observes, "A church planting movement is a rapid and exponential increase of indigenous churches planting churches within a given people group or population segment."[1] If a people group is found on the Southern California beaches or in enclaves of ethnic groups in urban centers or in rural North America, it must be indigenously evangelized by churches planting new churches.

Church-planting movements are highly desirable, as they contribute greatly to kingdom growth. Church-planting movements result in large numbers of people coming into authentic relationship with Jesus and getting connected to vibrant faith communities. Garrison addresses the importance of church planting movements:

"So why is a church planting movement so special? Because it seems to hold forth the greatest potential for the largest number of lost individuals glorifying God by coming into a new life in Christ and entering into communities of faith."[2]

Garrison's research reveals that church-planting movements are highly desirable if the Great Commission is to be fulfilled and God's kingdom radically expanded. A genuine church-planting movement is much more than adding a smattering of churches to those that already exist. The act of raising up, equipping, and sending out church planters to start churches within communities and people groups, in and of itself, is not necessarily a movement. It is church planting, but it is not a planting movement.

To begin a church-planting movement, we need trained and deployed planters. We need to start more and more churches. However, until the vision of church planting embeds itself into the core of our local churches, we are just dabbling in multiplication, not starting a movement. We are dancing at the fringe of a movement but not in the midst of one. "A church planting movement is not simply an increase in the number of churches, even though this also is positive," says Garrison. "A church planting movement occurs when the vision of churches planting churches spreads from the missionary and professional church planter *into the churches themselves, so that by their very nature* they are winning the lost and reproducing themselves."[3] Garrison's insights are gleaned from church-planting movements that he has observed on the mission field.

Are such movements possible in North America? This is a critical consideration as we evaluate the ability of churches to plant churches in a North American culture. If the North American church relentlessly pursued the starting of churches, could a movement be birthed? Might a radical expansion of God's redemptive power in the diversity of the twenty-first century be possible?

Historically, there are indicators that such a movement can occur. Roger Finke and Rodney Stark, in their book *The Churching of America 1776–1990*, note how the Methodists and Baptists made great strides in reaching eighteenth-century America through church planting. It is a misnomer that religion in the colonial era was highly embraced. "The vast majority of Americans had not been reached by an organized faith."[4] Many religious groups simply settled in and were content with the status quo. Their clergy rested in their comfort zones. They simply fed their spiritual flocks. They mused on theological topics. They rubbed shoulders with powerbrokers. They dallied in intellectual gymnastics. In contrast, as Finke and Stark point out, there were those who "had fire in their bellies and brimstones on their minds."[5] The authors expand on this theme: "Established faiths had drawn such a tepid response from the population that few Americans were churched. Many of their clergy had indeed become 'men of learning and elegance,' who flocked to Harvard and Yale, scorning the 'arts of gaining proselytes.' But upstart forces stirred. Rough and ready itinerants were on the prowl, men who firmly believed that the whole world was to be saved.[6] It was these groups that were compelled to expand the gospel presence.

The Methodists were on the forefront of this expansion. Their hearts were stirred. They pushed into the fringe of society. They ventured out to the frontiers:

The major shift in the American religious market in this period was the meteoric rise of Methodism. In 1776 the

Methodists were a tiny religious society with only [sixty-five] churches scattered through the colonies. Seven decades later they towered over the nation. In 1850 there were 13,302 Methodist congregations, enrolling more than 2.6 million members—the largest single denomination, accounting for more than a third of all American church members. For such growth to occur in eighty years seems nearly miraculous. But the general histories of American religion would make it even more of a miracle. Because all agree that religion fell into a state of sad neglect in the wake of the American Revolution, they would confine the rise of Methodism to less than fifty years.[7]

They went to people, sharing the life-changing message of faith. This resulted in incredible growth of churches and what amounted to a church-planting movement.

Moving from sixty-five congregations to over thirteen thousand is evidence of church-planting effectiveness. The Methodists engaged their culture. They presented a gospel that would intersect with people's lives. They were Great Commission-minded. They were going and making disciples. They were not content with inviting folks into existing structures and buildings.

These leaders were passionate about spreading the gospel message. They went to highways and byways. They went on horseback. They preached in season and out of season. They clearly, simply, and tirelessly communicated the gospel. And people responded. Lives were changed. Churches were started. The Methodists were missional in their approach as they moved beyond their church doors into the outdoors.

Over time, however, their evangelistic tenacity began to erode. They settled into the comfortable confines of the acceptable clergy. A clergy that was professional but no longer passionate. A clergy that was efficient but no longer evangelistic. A clergy that labored for the established church but no longer leveraged opportunities to empower new churches. Finke and Stark underscore this when they say, "Evangelism is no longer *the* mission of the church, the 'adequacy' of sanctification is questioned, and the clear boundaries between Christian and non-Christian have faded."[8]

This is true today. Many leaders and churches have waned in their evangelistic fervor. Today's church has benefited from a previous generation's boldness to engage their culture and start new churches. We have an appreciation for this effort but little compulsion to duplicate it. We are content to pluck the fruit from the trees (churches) that our forebears have planted. We have no driving desire to plant new trees (churches), much less begin new orchards (a church-planting movement).

The institutionalization of the church has moved it from having a *fort* mentality to a *fortress* mentality. Instead of being on the edge of the frontier, pushing outward, we stay safely within our four walls, protecting what we have already gained. The church that once addressed and challenged the culture now accommodates and cherishes the culture. "The institution, which first ascended out of the culture," say Ed Stetzer and David Garrison, "eventually became acclimated to the culture and lost its impulse for meaningful, evangelistic engagement."[9] Preservation has become more important to us than proclamation. Acceptance has become more important to today's church than evangelistic aggressiveness. Church planting is a secondary priority, as it is viewed as disrupting the delicate balance between the church and the culture.

The ministry dollars that it takes to do church in North America can be referred to as the *ecclesionomics* of the church. Facility needs, staff compensation, and program support are the big three economic realities of most existing churches. The existing church views itself as its economic priority. Starting new churches would put a dent into its available dollars. Stetzer and Garrison state it this way: "The paradigmatic weakness is that we can't do many things because of the limiting nature of ecclesionomics. Starting new churches would be like creating competitors. That's like sending your tithers and their tithes right out the door. This potential reality becomes a huge disincentive for the traditional church paradigm, which impedes the development of movements."[10] These observations regarding the North American church and church-planting movements place the local church squarely in a pivotal position for church expansion. Churches planting churches will drive a church-planting movement.

Tom Steffen noted the important role that the local church played in planting churches in the Philippines. Evangelism adds believers, but church planting multiplies kingdom growth. Church planting moves the gospel into unreached areas:

Evangelism works upon the premise of addition. Churches grow by adding new believers to the rolls. Church planting, however, works upon the premise of multiplication! New church plants not only add new believers to the rolls, they launch generations of outreach patterns with the potential of winning multitudes to the Lord. Effective church plants are dynamic in that they effectively evangelize an area, while at the same time establish a base from which to launch new church planters, so that the cycle can begin again in other unchurched areas. Effective Christian workers will seek to church areas, rather than to merely evangelize them.[11]

New churches are bases of evangelistic endeavors. They are the jumping-off points into yet-to-be-reached areas.

Whether it is in the two-thirds world or in North American culture, the necessity of the existing church to multiply must be elevated. Leaders and churches have to be swayed from their kingdom competitiveness ("My church is doing a better job than the church across town") to a kingdom competency ("I best please God when I move his kingdom forward"). "Until our ultimate goal is to please God and not our peers," say the authors of *Spin-Off Churches*, "the church planting movement will be hampered."[12]

In his book *Be Fruitful and Multiply*, Robert Logan makes the argument that multiplication movements can happen anywhere, as long as a proper approach is taken: "Church multiplication movements can happen anywhere, anytime. They adapt to the culture, they raise leaders from the harvest, and they build multiplication into the genetic code."[13] He highlights three key ingredients needed to ignite such a movement: First, multiplication movements are empowered by God. "Supernatural involvement is necessary. Whenever you see a multiplication movement, God has to show up."[14] Second, multiplication movements are culturally relevant: "They must connect to the hearts of people. For lives to be changed, the needs of the people must be addressed and met."[15] And third, multiplication movements use reproducible methods: "Reproducibility is the cornerstone of any successful church multiplication movement."[16]

Can there be a church-planting movement in the West? Can the exponential expansion of God's kingdom be experienced in North America? The answer is yes! If the church can recapture the spirit of the Great Commission, it will engage in church planting. If the church repurposes its mission for reaching the lost, it will engage in church planting. If the church stops neglecting those outside their walls as a result of inside-the-walls selfishness, it will engage in church planting.

Catapulting a parenting dream into a movement is the destiny to which kingdom-conscious leaders should aspire. Creating a movement will take plenty of heart—the heart to regularly participate in church-parenting endeavors, the heart to take more and more territory for God by creating reproducing churches, the heart to recruit other church leaders to join in sending ripples to the other shore.

Between each planting effort, there will be a recovery time, but never allow your congregation to lose sight of the vision for church multiplication. Most healthy churches can and should reproduce every three to four years. By doing so, we will ensure that our legacy will outlive us. The churches we help parent will become living monuments to the grace of God in the lives of people. Do not fall short of the incredible plan God has for his church.

APPENDIXES

PARENT CHURCH RESOURCES

APPENDIX
1

CREATING A PARENT ACTION PLAN: RETREAT GUIDELINE

PLANNING FOR THE RETREAT

SET-UP

You will want the room in which you hold your retreat to be arranged in a way that encourages group interaction and community building. The most desirable arrangement is to have participants seated around round tables. If round tables are not available, rectangular tables can be set up in such a way that four to eight people can sit around them, facing each other.

MATERIALS

You will need workbooks, pens, nametags, a projector, a whiteboard or chalkboard, and a flip chart.

SCHEDULE

Pre-event	8:30–9:00 a.m.
Introduction, Overview of Day, Prayer	9:00–9:30 a.m.
Session I: Laying a Foundation for Church Planting	9:30–10:30 a.m.
Break	10:30–10:45 a.m.
Session II: Current Reality	10:45–11:45 a.m.
Lunch	11:45 a.m.–12:30 p.m.
Session III: Cast the Vision	12:30–1:00 p.m.
Session IV: Craft an Action Plan, part 1 (prayer, team development, location identification, selection of church planter/leader)	1:00–2:30 p.m.
Break	2:30–2:45 p.m.
Session V: Craft an Action Plan, part 2 (methodology, budget, launch team recruitment philosophy, core team commissioning)	2:45–3:45 p.m.
Session VI: Care for the Parent (recovery)	3:45–4:00 p.m.
Session VII: Continue to Multiply (reproduction)	4:00–4:30 p.m.

GETTING THE DAY STARTED

PRE-EVENT

Half an hour prior to the event, make sure that coffee, water, and juice is available at each table. It is also suggested that you put out food. We are a social people. Interacting around food and drink sets a tone in which people can enjoy conversation, community, and a relaxed environment. As people arrive, invite them to be seated at the tables and to spend the first half hour of their day visiting together.

INTRODUCTION, OVERVIEW, PRAYER

Call for the group's attention, and ask each person participating in the retreat to share the following: his or her name, the church he or she represents, his or her ministry role, and where the person believes he or she is in the parenting process.

Share with the individuals gathered that the purpose of this day is to help church teams develop a first-draft action plan for parenting a new church. The term *parent* will refer to an existing church that is participating in the starting of a new church. Although there are a variety of parent methodologies that can be employed in starting a new church, the emphasis in this retreat will be on daughtering.

In the context of this event, *daughtering* will be defined as a local congregation initiating and leading in the parenting of a new church. This means one church investing its time, energy, and resources in the starting of another church. The parent church may develop strategic partnerships to achieve its end result, but it will not be dependent on these partnerships to realize its parent vision.

Take a few moments to pray before beginning the training for the day.

SESSION I: LAYING A FOUNDATION FOR CHURCH PLANTING

FOUR ASSUMPTIONS

There are four underlying assumptions that we need to make about a church that wants to carry out this parent action plan.

1. The pastor is called to lead his or her church in this endeavor. It is difficult to lead a church in starting a church. There will be challenging times as people begin to respond to the opportunity to help plant this new work. Key leaders will be called out from the parent church to participate in the core team of the daughter church. Dollars will follow this plant. This work is not for the faint-of-heart leader. There will come a time in this process when the leader will have to be reminded that God has called him or her to do this, regardless of the cost.

2. The congregation wants to do this—they just don't know how. In order for a church to parent a church, the majority of the congregation must be fully in. Not everyone will agree with planting, but the key leaders must. This plan assumes that there is little, if any, convincing to be done. The focus is on developing the plan, not on getting the people onboard.

3. The church is healthy and fit. An unhealthy, ill-fit church can multiply, but it will typically produce an unhealthy, ill-fit church. If you are not sure as to your church's health, it is suggested that you take your church through some form of church health assessment.

4. The timing is right. Timing is a huge factor in parenting a church. There is no ideal time to parent, but there are times that are better than others.

Which, if any, of these assumptions are not true of your church? How might you address false assumptions you have about your church?

FOUR INDICATORS THAT NOW MAY NOT BE THE BEST TIME TO PLANT

1. Your church is going through a major change (relocation, a building project, a pastoral transition, etc.).

2. Your church is spiritually immature (has an ingrown attitude, is in a disagreement over fringe issues, etc.).

3. Your church has a large number of underdeveloped leaders.

4. Your church lacks reproducing systems.

If any of these indicators are in play, consideration should be given to waiting some time before you parent. This does not mean that you cannot begin some form of planning now, but your plan may need to be extended. An extended planning time will provide your church an opportunity to address these issues.

Which, if any, of these indicators are in play at this time for your church? How might you address the indicators?

GOD GAP

(Note to Retreat Facilitator: The God gap is a principle that will encourage church leaders to move ahead when they meet times of faith challenges. It is a heads up to the parent church leaders that God will fill the gaps between where they are and where they are going.)

"You can go anywhere from where you are." The God gap is where our resources stop and God's must start. We must arrive at this place if we are ever going to succeed. The church that chooses to parent a new church will live in this gap. Regardless of the planning done, every parent church will have to forge ahead in faith. This is a good thing. We must never get to the point that God is factored out of the equation.

(Note to Retreat Facilitator: The following verses are shared as an example of what will happen to those leaders and churches who step into the God gap. Peter walking on the water is an example of a God gap adventure. When he swung his leg over the side of the boat and stepped onto the water, his resources were no longer useful and God's resources were necessary for him to succeed at walking on water.)

1. Step into things you have never experienced before (see Matt. 14:29). What had Peter never done before? Walk on water. When a church moves toward parenting a new congregation, they will discover their God gap. They may not walk on water, but they will have incredible experiences they would never have apart from being in the gap.

2. Experience the touch of Jesus like you never have before (see Matt. 14:31). When Peter began to sink, he yelled out for Jesus. Immediately, Jesus reached out and grabbed his hand. Peter had been touched by Jesus multiple times, but never like this. He experienced the touch of Jesus in desperate circumstances. Parent church leaders will have these same types of encounters. They will experience the presence and touch of Jesus like never before. Why? They will be desperate enough they will need to.

THE NEHEMIAH PRINCIPLE

(Note to Retreat Facilitator: Ultimately, a new congregation must be birthed through a time of prayer. Parenting a new church based on believing it would be a good idea, pressure to do so, or being motivated by some external source is not enough. If God does not birth this in the leadership of the parent church, it will be short-lived. Nehemiah is an example of a leader who allowed God to solidify a burden to act in his heart.)

"When I heard these things, I sat down and wept. For some days I mourned and fasted and prayed before the God of heaven" (Neh. 1:4 NIV). Nehemiah was well aware of the Jerusalem challenge. He knew there was trouble. He was aware the walls had been torn down and the gates destroyed. His initial response could have been to rally others to join him in going to Jerusalem and addressing this problem. Instead he "mourned and fasted and prayed." Here are two principles for parent church leaders that can be taken from Nehemiah.

1. It is in prayer that burdens are birthed and plans are prepared. Nehemiah prayed to discern what, if anything, God wanted to do.

2. Prayer should saturate the whole effort of starting a new church. Leaders, begin your endeavor with prayer. Do we need new churches? Yes! Do we need existing churches to birth new churches? Yes! But need does not constitute burden; and burden can only be birthed in prayer.

FIVE Cs OF AN ACTION PLAN

(Note to Retreat Facilitator: A goal of this retreat is to develop a first draft parent action plan. The five steps below make up the key areas of an action plan, and they will make up the bulk of this retreat. Each will be developed in the following sessions.)

There are five steps to creating an action plan, which we call the five Cs. We will work through each of these steps as we move through our day.

- Current Reality
- Cast the Vision
- Craft an Action Plan: Elements of the Action Plan
  ○ Prayer

- Team development
- Location identification
- Choice of church planter/leader
- Methodology of parenting
- Budget
- Launch team recruitment philosophy
- Core team commissioning
- Care for the Parent: Recovery
- Continue to Multiply: Reproduction

SESSION II: CURRENT REALITY

PREPARING THE LEADER

An established church is much more like a ship than a speedboat. A speedboat is maneuvered more fluidly than a ship. It is quick and changes course easily. A ship takes much more time to steer. It has to be slowed and then brought around and given a wide berth.

First, you must overcome your hesitance. The pastor is the key to embracing new vision. If you are willing to step out into church planting, your congregation will almost always be willing. If you are hesitant, your people will be hesitant. You will have to be a "salmon" leader—willing to leave your comfort zone and swim upstream. Doris Kearns Goodwin says, "At their best, all effective leaders, share a gift for defining a vision, for moving people toward a direction for the future."[1]

Second, resist the hindrance of "what gets rewarded is what gets done." The reality is that most denominations do not recognize or reward churches that parent. There are times when parenting is actually discouraged. The calculations of district assessments are often figured from the previous year's happenings. Some of the tithers from the previous year who moved their investment to a daughter church won't be in your church to help pay the next year's assessment, which will result in lower numbers on district assessments.

Third, beware of the three Bs: buildings, bodies, and budgets. Church leadership must protect themselves from making the three Bs the measure of the church's effectiveness. Paul Becker and Mark Williams say in their book, *The Dynamic Daughter Church Planting Handbook*, "It is easy for pastors to see the growth of their own churches as being their first and only priority. The more you have the three Bs, the more esteem you seem to have, both in the eyes of others and in your own eyes."[2] The leadership must view church planting as something that they value.

What do you see as the biggest personal obstacles in moving forward in parenting a church? What is your current indebtedness? How much do you currently give to missions? What size congregation do you believe you can pastor with your leadership style and gifts?

FIVE AREAS OF INVESTMENT
1. Members.
2. Money—core tithes plus parental gifts.
3. Mud—you will be giving up turf and territory.
4. Ministry resources—gifts, skills, and talents will be invested out.
5. Momentum—you will have a bit of a slowdown; plan for it and plan to overcome it.

Review the five areas of investment. List them in order of perceived difficulty for you from one to five (one being most difficult, five being least). Why did you rate them as you did? How could this inform your parenting plans?

EFFECTIVE PARENTING DIAGRAM

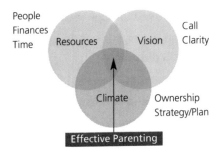

What resources does your church currently have in the way of people, finances, and time? How clear is your church's vision to parent? Describe the current receptivity of your church regarding planting a church.

SESSION III: CAST THE VISION

THE VALUE OF VISION

Vision leaks—you can't pour it in once and expect it to still be there later. In other words, a pastor cannot simply relate the vision to a congregation once and assume that the people will catch it, understand it, and fully embrace it. Understanding that vision can easily escape (leak) from the forefront of the parent congregation's thinking will inform how often the vision is cast and recast. Vision motivates people. Vision compels people to action. Vision draws people into the church-planting process.

VISION MANTRA

Say it often. Keep it simple. Let it burn. A vision understood is a vision pursued. Vision is cast in one-on-one conversations, via leadership meetings, and through preaching. It is the leader's responsibility to do all he or she can to ensure that the vision remains center stage in the church.

One-on-One Conversations. Be able to state your multiplication vision to an individual in one sentence. List ten people with whom you need to share your vision individually. When will you meet with these people? List several other people who can help you cast the vision.

Leadership Meetings. What leadership meetings do you have? How often do these meetings occur? How might you include vision casting in these meetings? What resources might you put into your leaders' hands in order to help them better understand the parenting and daughtering visions?

Preaching. What series can you preach to emphasize the church-planting vision? What biblical book can you preach to emphasize the vision? How often will you include the vision in your preaching? How might you track your messages to be sure that your goals are being met in this area?

SESSION IV: CRAFT AN ACTION PLAN, PART 1
(PRAYER, TEAM DEVELOPMENT, LOCATION IDENTIFICATION,
CHOICE OF CHURCH PLANTER/LEADER)

Jack Welch, author of *Winning*, says, "If you want to win, when it comes to strategy, ponder less and do more."[3]

One of the most effective means of planting missional churches is to have an established church give the new church life and vitality.

It is right and natural for churches to give birth to churches. Church multiplication requires no institution apart from existing churches. It does not depend on powerful leaders. Ordinary people in ordinary churches can do God's work when they are willing to simply pursue the Great Commission in the power of the Holy Spirit.

The pursuit of the Great Commission through the planting of missional churches, however, demands a plan. A friend of mine, Larry McKain, once told me, "A dream without a plan is a wish." It may be a leader's dream to daughter a church, but if a plan is not developed and implemented, this dream will only remain a wish.

A plan provides a roadmap to follow and a method of accountability. A plan will guide a church along a path that will end in the birth of a new missional church.

Goals are **NOT** the Strategy
Action Steps **ARE** the Strategy

PRAYER

Prayer is foundational for the parenting of a church. It is in prayer that burdens are birthed and plans are prepared. The willingness to pray for the church-planting effort is critical to the effectiveness of new missional outposts.

We tend to do our work and then trust that God will bless it. We plan things out, believing that God will redirect us if we're heading the wrong way. And God does direct as we move. We see this in the wise words of Solomon: "Commit your actions to the LORD, and your plans will succeed" (Prov. 16:3) and "We can make our plans, but the LORD determines our steps" (16:9).

A genuine prayer dependency needs to wrap itself around our plans for parenting. Can a church parent apart from prayer? Yes! But it parents much more effectively with prayer.

Recruit a prayer team for the sole purpose of praying for church-planting opportunities. There are people in your church who are particularly gifted to pray. Recruit them to a church-planting prayer team. Keep them informed as to planting needs. Give them the names of potential planters (those who might be suited to be the daughter church's pastor). Provide a list of communities in which a new church might be started or is already starting. List the names of potential intercessors. Contact these people, and recruit them to the church-planting prayer team. Ask them, "When will you contact these people? When will you meet with them? Who will coordinate the plans?"

Begin to prayer-walk through your community, looking for specific locations in which a new church might be started. Enlist a group of people who might come together on a Saturday and simply walk through parts of your community. This will increase these individuals' awareness of the community that surrounds your church.

TEAM DEVELOPMENT (BUILDING A PARENT ACTION TEAM)

A parent action team is critical to the development of your parent plan. Proverbs speaks to the wisdom of working in teams: "Get all the advice and instruction you can, so you will be wise the rest of your life" (Prov. 19:20). "Commit yourself to instruction; listen carefully to words of knowledge" (23:12).

This parent action team will assist in determining the method and development of the strategy for parenting a new multiplying church.

When creating this team, you will need to: develop a profile for an ideal team member, decide how many team members will be needed, write a ministry description for team members, clarify team members' roles, recruit people.

Team Profile. Build this profile based on your needs for this team. Suggested attributes of a team member would be that he or she is a team player, a strategic thinker, respected in the congregation, a big-picture thinker, and someone who has a heart for the local community. List the attributes you want to look for in a team member. Determine the size of the parent team. Think about who you would like to have for a team leader.

Ministry Description. This should include: to whom the team will be accountable, what will be expected of the team, and how long the members will be needed to serve.

Role Clarification. This team will be involved in considering the church's parenting model, potential church-planting locations, finances, timing of the plant, selection of a church planter, and communication of progress to the congregation.

Next Steps. Develop a ministry description and an expectation list for parent team members. Get input from key leaders. Make a list of people who meet the criteria for a parent team member (have several more individuals on the list than the number of people you will actually need). Prayerfully pare down the list. Meet with each person on the list individually. Share with each person the ministry description for a team member. Give people time to consider (not more than a week). Get back to each individual. Once a team is in place, set the first meeting date, time, and location.

LOCATION IDENTIFICATION

The exact location of the new church plant should be determined by the planter, but the team should discuss several locations to which members feel drawn for beginning a new church.

Identify locations in which a church might be planted. Then ask:

- How were these locations identified?
- What opportunities does each one provide for church planting?
- What research will be needed to provide current information on these locations?
- Who will do this research?
- When will it be done?
- In what format will it be reported?

SELECTION OF CHURCH PLANTER/LEADER

It is imperative that when parenting a church, the parent recruits a church planter who it can support with enthusiasm. Keep several things in mind when seeking a church planter: Be aware of the characteristics of effective planters; know where to find "fishing pools" for potential planters; make sure that the planter has applied the three key preparatory components: assessment, training, and coaching (these will be covered below); and measure the potential planters' motives for wanting to plant.

Characteristics of an Effective Planter. Educate yourself in the character traits of an effective church planter. In church-planting circles, thirteen characteristics have been identified as key traits in effective church planters. A successful church planter:

- Has visionary capacity. This is the ability to imagine the future and persuade others to join his or her vision.
- Is intrinsically motivated. This person is a self-starter.
- Creates ownership of ministry. He or she trains leaders to reproduce leaders.
- Relates to the unchurched. This person easily shares Christ and interacts well with the spiritually disconnected.
- Manages family well. His or her marriage partner is just as called as the church planter.
- Effectively builds relationships. A successful planter initiates and builds relationships with others.
- Is committed to church growth. This person implements healthy church growth principles.
- Is responsive to the community. He or she adapts ministry to the culture and to the target group.
- Utilizes the giftedness of others. An effective church planter equips and releases people into ministry based on their giftedness.
- Is flexible and adaptable. He or she adjusts to surprises and handles ambiguity well.
- Builds a cohesive church body. This person manages a team toward shared goals and priorities.

- Is resilient and determined. He or she bounces back from setbacks.
- Exercises faith. A successful planter translates personal convictions into ministry initiatives.

What has been your exposure to these characteristics to date? How will you further educate yourself in these characteristics?

Planter Fishing Pools. Some areas to find an effective church planter are: youth pastors, assistant or associate pastors of large churches, senior pastors looking for a new challenge, seminary students, entrepreneurial business leaders, church planters who are five years or more into their existing plant, para-church organizations (such as, Navigators, Campus Crusade, Young Life, Youth for Christ), missionaries, early retired laity, or compatible denominations.

Which of the fishing pools listed here do you feel provides the best resource for you? What are some other pools you feel might be productively used?

Three Critical Components for a Church Planter to Embrace. Three preparatory components are essential in order for a church planter to be of the highest quality. These components are assessment, training, and coaching.

Each of these steps should be nonnegotiable when selecting a planter. The parent-church leadership must insist that none of these are short-circuited.

First, assessment is a formal process by which a potential planter is vetted using the thirteen characteristics highlighted above. There are a variety of organizations that provide such an assessment process. Many denominations, as well, provide excellent ones.

When you look for an assessment process to utilize, search for a process that is based on the thirteen characteristics of an effective planter and has the following qualities: a psychological evaluation, behavioral interviews, a spousal assessment, and interactive team-building exercises. Do not consider a potential planter unless he or she has already been assessed or is willing to be assessed.

To what assessments do you have access? How will you utilize these assessments?

Second, training is required for the development of a plan for planting a church. The development of the church-planting plan is ultimately the responsibility of the planter, not of the parent church. However, there are many organizations that help equip planters in this plan development. It is recommended that the parent church help the planter in finding and selecting such an organization. It is suggested that the parent church underwrite any cost associated in the development of this plan.

Elements of an effective church-planting plan include: development of mission, vision, and core values; marketing of the new church; budget development; securing of a location for the new church; strategies for contextualizing ministry to the community in which the church will be planted; a timeline as well as critical milestones to be reached along the way; style of ministry; and a plan to multiply.

What training systems are available to you? How might you ensure that your planter participates in these?

Third, coaching is the establishing of a relationship between a planter and another person who might keep him or her accountable for the development and implementation of the church-planting plan.

The parent-church pastor should not coach the planter. It is difficult for a parent pastor not to impose on the planter his or her own way of doing ministry.

The goal of an excellent coach is to help the planter implement the plan. He or she asks good questions. The coach holds the planter highly accountable and communicates the planter's progress to the parent church. A coaching relationship ought to last for a minimum of twelve months, but it is encouraged that it be an eighteen-month relationship.

How will you ensure competent and reliable coaching for your planter? What expectations will you have of the coach for relating to you as the parent church? What role will you as the parent pastor play in the coaching process?

Motives of a Church Planter. There are many motives a person may have for wanting to plant a church. A planter's primary motive should be that of wanting to reach more people for Christ.

When selecting a planter to partner with your church, be leery of those who: have a strong desire to preach but who have not been given opportunities to do so; feel frustrated in their present situations because they are unable to do what they want to do; have no opportunity to pastor an established church; have something to prove; look at planting as an opportunity to practice ministerial skills; or want to do church the "right" way.

What steps will you take to test the motives of your planter? What is your motive in parenting?

Next Steps in Selecting a Church Planter/Leader. Review the thirteen characteristics of an effective planter. Determine the assessment process you will use for potential planters. Review the planter fishing pools. To which fishing pools do you have access? Which fishing pools will you explore? How will you train your planter? How will you connect your planter to a coach? When do you want to have your planter in place?

SESSION V: CRAFT AN ACTION PLAN, PART 2 (METHODOLOGY, BUDGET, LAUNCH TEAM RECRUITMENT PHILOSOPHY, CORE TEAM COMMISSIONING)

METHODOLOGY (DETERMINE A PLANTING/PARENTING SYSTEM)

There are a variety of parenting methods a church might employ. The leadership will need to determine which methodology it feels is best for their church.

Review the following descriptions. Discuss each one. Place a check next to the ones you prefer.

- Daughter. One church takes on the primary task of sending out a core group of people with a planter in order to begin a new church.
- Shared Partnership. Two churches join together to spearhead the planting of a new reproducing church.
- Satellite. A local church meets in multiple locations with the intent that each group will become a fully organized reproducing church. Goal markers are put in place for each group (for example, financial strength, attendance, leadership structure), and when reached by a group, it spins off as an independent church.
- Multi-Site. A local church meets in multiple locations as one church.

- Language Group Congregations. A church of one ethnic group begins a church through targeting another ethnic group with a language other than its own.
- House Church. A congregation begins a group meeting in a home. This group doesn't expand beyond the home but multiplies other house churches.
- Adoption. A local church adopts an existing congregation into its family.
- Surrogate. A local church provides a "womb" in which a new congregation can grow and develop.
- Next Paradigm. The church plan that God is birthing in the heart of both a leader and a local church that has yet to be implemented.

List the top three methodologies that you would be willing to utilize. Select the methodology you will use. Discuss why this is the best methodology for your church. Outline the strategy you will use to share this system with the congregation.

BUDGET

Daughtering a church demands a financial investment. The earlier a church begins to prepare for this, the better. The following formula may help with this: consistent investment plus extended time equals increased resources.

Two foundational principles must be built on in your preparation process: First, you must ask your people to invest boldly in planting; and second, your people will give to a vision that they embrace.

Finances are not a problem. What matters in motivating a congregation is the boldness and vision of its leadership. When a congregation understands that planting a church is a genuine passion of its leader, and when it is seen that starting a new church is an extension of the leader's vision, it will respond.

Seven ideas for preparing to finance a church planting endeavor are:

- Build church planting into your annual budget.
- Make church planting part of the missions budget.
- Develop special projects in your church to collect funds for planting.
- Creatively find monies in the church budget (such as, give a tithe of each month's offering, tithe the surplus of any residual budget dollars, invest the entire offering from the last Sunday of the year to this fund, tithe the fifth Sunday offerings).
- Tithe special gifts.
- Set up a church-planting memorial fund.
- Encourage end-of-year giving toward church planting.

How much funding will you need to help start a new church? What will you do to set money aside for this? When will you begin to do this? Who in your church could oversee this financing strategy? Which key people may personally invest in this vision? How will you handle core tithes?

LAUNCH TEAM RECRUITMENT PHILOSOPHY

This recruitment strategy has to do with how the parent church will allow the planter to recruit people as a part of the new church's core team.

Conflict can easily arise between a planter and a parent church if the strategy a planter is to use is not clearly laid out.

This strategy needs to be developed on the front end and clearly communicated to the planter.

It is imperative that the parent church fulfills whatever commitments it makes to the planter. Therefore, be sure that you allow the planter to do whatever you have told the person that he or she can do.

Here are four questions for which the parent-church task force should develop answers:

1. In what ways can the planter recruit team members from the parent church? Are you going to give the planter access to the pulpit and the platform? Will the planter be able to connect with small groups and Sunday school classes or have other opportunities that might give him or her exposure to the people of the congregation? Can the planter share his or her planting dream in membership classes?

2. Who can the planter recruit? Can the planter recruit anyone? Are all church members available for him or her to recruit? What about staff members? Are there any families in the parent church that are off limits?

3. When can the planter recruit? Does the planter have a time frame in which to recruit? Is he or she able to recruit right up to the launch? Or is there a window of opportunity (for example, a four-month period) that the planter needs to function within?

4. Where can the planter recruit? Is the planter free to recruit whenever, wherever, and however he or she chooses? Is he or she limited to on-property recruitment? Weekend services? Is the planter able to make appointments with church members and to have recruitment conversations?

When will you walk through these questions? What other questions do these ones spawn in your mind? What do you believe your recruitment strategy will be? Are you comfortable with the recruitment strategy you have developed? What communication system will you employ to make sure that the planter understands your recruitment parameters? How will you communicate with members of the congregation that they should be open to going and helping to begin this new work?

CORE TEAM COMMISSIONING

The sending of the planter and the team that he or she has recruited from the parent church should be a high day in the life of the church. To ensure that this is indeed a celebrated occasion, it needs to be well planned and thought out. This commission should be marked by: celebrating, honoring, and modeling.

An Atmosphere of Celebration. When a new baby is brought into the world, his or her day of birth is typically a day of much joy, laughter, and celebration. The day that the church planter and his or her team is released needs to embody such an atmosphere.

This celebration ought to include: the planter, sharing her or his vision for the new church; testimonies from some of the core-team members; a presentation of the planting community; a commissioning rite; a commissioning prayer; a vision-casting sermon by the parent pastor for future plants; and a reception for mingling, relating, hugging, and for encouraging farewells. These are just a few suggestions. Use innovation. Decorate your sanctuary to reflect a celebratory atmosphere. Video record the service to use for future vision-casting opportunities.

Honor a Changing Relationship. The new church that you plant will, most likely, not look like you, the parent church. Honor this. Communicate that this new child will be like you, but it will not be you. Affirm the unique style that this new work will reflect.

Model a Healthy Parent-Child Relationship. It is difficult for parents to let go of their children. It will be no different for a church parent. Releasing a core of people to go and start a new church will be an emotional experience. Do not underestimate this. It will be hard, but it will be worth it. Remind yourself to let go. Allow this new church the freedom to be what God has called it to be.

Develop an outline for the commissioning service. Who will oversee the details of this event? How can you appropriately honor this new church?

SESSION VI: CARE FOR THE PARENT (RECOVERY)

RECOVERY FOR THE LONG HAUL

Parent recovery is the ability of a parent church to recapture its financial, emotional, and leadership momentum after a new church launch. Much as a mother must have time to recover after the birth of a child, so a parent church must prepare for its recovery. A healthy recovery will provide strength for multiplying (giving birth) at another time in the future.

This recovery process does not begin after the new church's team has been commissioned; it begins at the time of conception. A woman who takes care of herself prior to and during her pregnancy will typically have a faster rate of recovery after she gives birth than a woman who neglected her own care. It was my experience when our church parented other churches that we underestimated the recovery process. Looking back, we needed better care for the parent church.

A parent church that is most leveraged for a quick recovery is one that is actively evangelizing, growing, assimilating, developing new givers, and raising up new leaders even as they work toward a church plant. Keep these priorities as an emphasis, and you will find that recovery after a church plant will happen at a quicker pace.

ATTENDANCE RECOVERY

It can take between six and eighteen months to recover from birthing a church if 10 percent of your average attendance goes with the new church. This assumes that the parent church is involved in effective outreach and assimilation. Lack of recovery in regard to attendance is often an indication of weak evangelism and assimilation systems in the parent church.

Preparation for recovering attendance after a church plant is done by being aggressive, strategic, and intentional in evangelism methodology before, during, and after your new church is birthed.

Evaluate your existing assimilation process. How have you been at encouraging people to remain in the church? what changes might you make to increase effectiveness in this area?

How many members are you projecting will go with the new church? What percentage of your average attendance is this number? How much will you need to grow to replace those people you are investing? Detail your evangelistic strategy. Evaluate and adjust your assimilation strategy.

FINANCIAL RECOVERY

The time required for recovering financially will vary depending on the number of tithers who were invested into the new church. If your church has chosen to invest additional dollars into the plant above and beyond giving away its core tithers, this will also impact financial recovery.

There are several strategies that a parent church can employ to prepare for financial recovery:

- Create an emergency fund that is invested in regularly as the plant is being ramped up.
- Recruit key givers to pledge dollars above and beyond their normal giving for twelve months following the commissioning service.
- Develop a stewardship emphasis to be presented within one month of the commissioning service.
- Have the daughter church reinvest into the parent church a predesignated amount within three years after its launch.
- Take up special offerings on each fifth Sunday leading up to the commissioning service.

Creativity is your only limitation. Strategize, interact with ideas, and prepare for the financial challenges you will have after planting your daughter church.

What is the average amount of giving that will be invested in the new church through core tithes? How much are you investing in the plant above the core tithes? What methodology will you employ to prepare now for future financial challenges?

LEADERSHIP RECOVERY

It can take six to eighteen months to raise up new leaders to replace those you invested in the planting mission. This amount of time can be curtailed through a leadership development process. Look for ways to improve your church's system of challenging, training, and mobilizing people for ministry.

Questions you need to consider: What are you currently doing to develop new leaders? What process do you have in place for existing leaders to mentor emerging leaders? What is the pastor doing to invest in both existing and emerging leaders? What process is in place to help existing leaders multiply themselves?

How many existing leaders do you project might commit to the new church? What might you do to help the existing leaders reproduce themselves in others? How are you identifying potential leaders? Outline your leadership development plan. When will you implement this plan?

SESSION VII: CONTINUE TO MULTIPLY (REPRODUCTION)

A healthy church ought to be able to daughter a church every three to five years. This will only be done, however, if the parent church sees planting as multiplication and not merely addition. When the recovery systems are in place, and the leadership affirms multiplication as a value of their evangelistic heart, then one church planted will not be sufficient. Determine to build a multiplication mind-set into the congregation you lead.

George Bullard, congregational and denominational strategic leadership coach, gives a good example of this:

During the generation following World War II, a major denomination started a new congregation in a region of the country where they had never had congregations before. . . . From the beginning this was a reproducing congregation. It would regularly send out groups from within its congregation to start new congregations throughout the region. It would also sponsor, nest, or adopt new congregations of its denomination that began to emerge from other efforts.

More than fifty years since the start of this congregation, almost [three hundred] congregations of the denomination exist within a fifty-mile radius of where this congregation started. More than 80 percent of the congregations are primarily composed of non-Anglo Americans, making this one of the most culturally diverse regions of this denomination in North America.[4]

This story illustrates what can happen when a church and its leadership catch a vision for its region and invest themselves in the starting of new churches. A church willing to give permission to its people to participate in the starting of new congregations will see fruit beyond its wildest dreams.

What is your viewpoint of church multiplication as opposed to church addition? Identify several areas in which you might plant churches. Identify several subgroups that you may not be reaching well with your current ministry. Discuss a methodology to move your church beyond its first church plant to future planting.

TEN MISTAKES MADE IN PARENTING A NEW CHURCH

1. Moving ahead before the congregation has ownership.

2. Making a poor church planter selection.

3. Failing to create a parenting plan.

4. Rushing the developmental process.

5. Not giving the parent church time to recover after the church plant.

6. Putting strategy implementation before Spirit initiative.

7. Sanctifying deadlines.

8. Wanting to clone instead of parent.

9. Having an overbearing parent presence in the life of the daughter church.

10. Cutting the daughter off immediately after it leaves the womb.

APPENDIX 3

EIGHT GUIDELINES FOR RELATING TO A PARENT CHURCH

1. Communication. It is the responsibility of the planter, the daughter-church pastor, to keep the parent church informed as to the progress of the plant. Find out which methods the parent church desires you to communicate back to it. Hint: You cannot overcommunicate.

2. Loyalty. Speak positively about your parent. Even if there are issues that you are not overly thrilled about, never air these publicly. You are part of a team. Make sure no one can second-guess where your loyalties lie. Hint: Loyalty will always result in long-term effectiveness.

3. Play by the Rules. Make sure you understand what the parent will allow you to do and how it will allow you to do it. If the parent will allow you to recruit core members, make sure you know its recruitment rules. If the parent will allow you to raise funds, make sure you know its fund-raising rules. Hint:

Never make up your own rules, and never stretch the parent's rules.

4. Honor Your Parent. Find methods of giving back to your parent. One church that was parented sent flowers to its "mom" on Mother's Day. Hint: Small tokens of appreciation go a long way.

5. Be Available. Don't get so caught up in your church plant that you are not available to help at home when help is needed. You may have resources that can benefit the parent church. Hint: Be as generous with your resources as you hope your parent will be.

6. Invite Your Parent Over. When you have special events, send an invitation to "Mom." And keep an open invitation to those who were involved in your church's birth. Be sure that the parent church knows that it is welcome to visit anytime. Hint: Never underestimate the power of invitation.

7. Participate in Family Reunions. Do things together with the parent. Go out of your way to have your two congregations get together. Hint: Your presence means a great deal to the parent.

8. Have Grandchildren. Better than being a parent is being a grandparent. Make sure you give this gift to your parent. And let your child know its grandparent. Hint: Don't let the family tree die.

NAVIGATING PARENT-DAUGHTER RELATIONSHIPS

1. Get buy-in from the elders, leaders, and influencers of your church before you go forward with parenting a new church. It's not fair to the church planter or the potential church plant to have the whole project upended due to lack of buy-in from the church leadership.

2. Make sure that both of you (parent and daughter) play by the rules. Daughter, understand what the parent church will allow you to do and how they will allow you to do it. Parent, do what you say you will do. Fulfill your commitments.

3. Come up with a parent-daughter covenant that clearly lays out the parameters of the relationship and that each party signs. Never assume anything on either side. Assumptions result in misunderstanding and frustration.

4. Parent, be sure to block for your daughter when necessary. Stick up for your daughter church when it comes under any kind

of friendly fire. This kind of criticism often comes from other Christians who do not understand the unconventional tactics the church plant may be using to reach people. You can offer your daughter a credibility that they will not have on their own. This is a huge gift!

5. Commission those parent-church members who choose to go with the church plant. Just as Paul and Barnabas were commissioned in Acts 13, so you should commission those who are going out from your midst to start a new church. Celebrate them for making this bold and daring move!

6. If any of your original church members return to the parent church, greet them with kindness and graciousness. Many of those who go out to begin a new work will eventually return to the parent church. Make this transition easy for them. Thank them that they were willing to begin a new work. Welcome them as homecoming missionaries.

7. Do all you can to help the daughter become a river instead of a lake. Stagnant water loses its freshness quickly.

8. It is unpleasant to be around a person with no sense of gratitude. Build a sense of gratitude into the church you help begin. This is best done by being gracious to your daughter.

9. Learn as much as you can from your first church-planting experience so that you can plant again from an experiential base. The wisdom you gain from your first planting endeavor will greatly enhance the next one. When we get to the place at which we fully understand that church multiplication is the heart of God, we will do whatever it takes to continue being involved in the church planting process.

NOTES

CHAPTER 1

1. Joel Comiskey, "The State of the North American Church," *Journal of the American Society of Church Growth* 16, (Spring 2005): 79.

2. Ibid., 80.

3. Ibid., 81.

4. Mike Regele, *Robust Church Development: A Vision for Mobilizing Regional Bodies in Support of Missional Congregations* (Rancho Santa Margarita, Calif.: Percept Group, Inc., 2003), 33–34.

5. Ibid., 82.

6. Fred Herron, *Expanding God's Kingdom through Church Planting* (New York: Writer's Showcase/iUniverse, 2003), 47.

7. Lyle Schaller, *44 Questions for Church Planters* (Nashville: Abingdon, 1991), 28.

8. Elmer Towns, foreword to *Spin-Off Churches: How One Church Successfully Plants Another*, by Rodney Harrison, Tom Cheyney, and Don Overstreet (Nashville: B&H Academic, 2008), xi.

CHAPTER 2

1. Lou Holtz, *Winning Every Day: The Game Plan for Success* (New York: HarperBusiness, 1998), 107.

CHAPTER 3

1. Bruce R. Finn, "Small Churches Can Plant Churches" (DMin dissertation, Reformed Theological Seminary, May 26, 2000), 15.

2. Ibid., 17.

3. Fred Herron, *Expanding God's Kingdom through Church Planting* (New York: Writer's Showcase/iUniverse, 2003), 8.

4. Ibid., 10.

CHAPTER 4

1. C. Peter Wagner, *Church Planting for a Greater Harvest: A Comprehensive Guide* (Ventura, Calif.: Regal, 1990), 19.

2. Bill Sheeks, *How to Plant a Church of God: Positive Guidelines for Action* (Cleveland, Tenn.: Pathway, 1987), xii.

3. David J. Hesselgrave, *Planting Churches Cross-Culturally: A Guide for Home and Foreign Missions* (Grand Rapids, Mich.: Baker, 1980), 33.

4. Elmer Towns, *Evangelism and Church Growth: A Practical Encyclopedia* (Ventura, Calif.: Regal, 1995), 97.

5. Ed Stetzer, *Planting Missional Churches: Planting a Church That's Biblically Sound and Reaching People in Culture* (Nashville: B&H Academic, 2006), 38.

6. Ibid., 41.

7. Paul Becker and Mark Williams, *The Dynamic Daughter Church Planting Handbook* (San Diego: Dynamic Church Planting International, 1999), 2.

8. Rodney Harrison, Tom Cheyney, and Don Overstreet, *Spin-Off Churches: How One Church Successfully Plants Another* (Nashville: B&H Academic, 2008), 32.

CHAPTER 5

1. Jill Rosenfeld, "Down-Home Food, Cutting-Edge Business," *Fast Company*, last modified March 31, 2000, http://www.fast company.com/39015/down-home-food-cutting-edge-business.

CHAPTER 6

1. C. Peter Wagner, *Church Planting for a Greater Harvest: A Comprehensive Guide* (Ventura, Calif.: Regal, 1990), 11.

2. For more information on the Church Multiplication Training Center, visit cmtcmultiply.org.

3. Lyle Schaller, *44 Questions for Church Planters* (Nashville: Abingdon, 1991), 27–28.

4. "Crime Does Not Pay," accessed June 28, 2013, http://therussler.tripod.com/dtps/stupid_criminals.html.

5. Michael Grondahl in Judith Ohikuare, "New Year, No Excuses: A Gym Lands New Members by Keeping It Simple," *Inc.* 35, no. 1 (February 2013): 22.

CHAPTER 7

1. Mike Regele, *Robust Church Development: A Vision for Mobilizing Regional Bodies in Support of Missional Congregations* (Rancho Santa Margarita, Calif.: Percept Group, Inc., 2003), 84.

2. J. Russell Crabtree, *The Fly in the Ointment: Why Denominations Aren't Helping Their Congregations and How They Can* (New York: Church Publishing, 2008), 80.

3. Ibid., 81.

4. Bob Roberts Jr., *The Multiplying Church: The New Math for Starting New Churches* (Grand Rapids, Mich.: Zondervan, 2008), 18.

5. Joel Comiskey, *Planting Churches That Reproduce* (Moreno Valley, Calif.: CCS, 2008), 21.

6. Tom A. Steffen, *Passing the Baton: Church Planting That Empowers* (La Habra, Calif.: Center for Organizational & Ministry Development, 1993), 164.

CHAPTER 8

1. Fred Herron, *Expanding God's Kingdom through Church Planting* (New York: Writer's Showcase/iUniverse, 2003), 51.

2. Roland Allen, *The Spontaneous Expansion of the Church: And the Causes That Hinder It* (Eugene, Ore.: Wipf & Stock, 1962), 7.

3. Edward Stetzer and Warren Bird, "The State of Church Planting in the United States: Research Overview and Qualitative Study of Primary Church Planting Entities," *Journal of the American Society for Church Growth* 19 (Summer 2008): 30.

4. Michael Estep, foreword to *Expanding Your Church's Mission: Sponsoring a New Church*, by Nina E. Beegle, ed. (Kansas City: Church of the Nazarene Extension Ministries), 3.

5. Neil Cole, *Organic Church: Growing Faith Where Life Happens* (San Francisco: Jossey-Bass, 2005), 109.

6. Joel Comiskey, *Planting Churches That Reproduce* (Moreno Valley, Calif.: CCS, 2008), 46.

7. For more information on the Crowded House Network, visit thecrowdedhouse.org.

8. Tim Thornborough in *Multiplying Churches: Reaching Today's Communities through Church Planting*, ed. Stephen Timmis (Ross-shire, Scotland: Christian Focus, 2000), 83.

9. Waldo J. Werning, *The Seed-Planting Church: Nurturing Churches to Health* (St. Charles, Ill.: ChurchSmart Resources, 2003), 41.

10. Charles Brock, *The Principles and Practice of Indigenous Church Planting* (Nashville: Broadman, 1981), 56.

11. Samuel D. Faircloth, *Church Planting for Reproduction* (Grand Rapids, Mich.: Baker, 1991), 178.

12. Rodney Harrison, *Seven Steps for Planting Churches* (Alpharetta, Ga.: North American Mission Board, SBC, 2004), 64.

13. Tom Nebel and Gary Rohrmayer, *Church Planting Landmines: Mistakes to Avoid in Year 2 through 10* (St. Charles, Ill.: ChurchSmart Resources, 2005), 140.

14. Aubrey Malphurs, *Planting Growing Churches for the 21st Century: A Comprehensive Guide for New Churches and Those Desiring Revival* (Grand Rapids, Mich.: Baker, 2004), 342.

15. Melvin Hodges, *A Guide to Church Planting* (Chicago: Moody, 1973), 94.

16. Carl Moorhous, *Growing New Churches: Step-by-Step Procedures in New Church Planting* (n.p.: Moorhous, 1975), 6.

17. Ralph Moore, *Let Go of the Ring: The Hope Chapel Story* (n.p.: Straight Street, 2000), 122.

18. Tom Nebel and Gary Rohrmayer, *How to Lead a Successful Church Planting Movement Workbook* (printed by authors, 2006), 9.

19. Bob Roberts, *The Multiplying Church: The New Math for Starting New Churches* (Grand Rapids, Mich.: Zondervan, 2008), 18.

20. Bob Roberts, *Transformation: How Glocal Churches Transform Lives and the World* (Grand Rapids, Mich.: Zondervan, 2006), 139.

CHAPTER 10

1. Floyd Tidsworth Jr., *Life Cycle of a New Congregation* (Nashville: Broadman, 1992), 16.

2. For more information on Dynamic Church Planting International, visit dcpi.org.

CHAPTER 12

1. For more information on knowing when your church is ready to parent, see Charles R. Ridley, *How to Select Church Planters: A Self-Study Inventory* (Pasadena, Calif.: Fuller Evangelistic Association, 1988).

2. To help churches refocus as to their identity and purpose, The Wesleyan Church offers a Church Planter Assessment Center. For more information, visit wesleyan.org/ecg/assessing.

CHAPTER 13

1. Training for developing parent action plans is available through New Church Specialties (newchurchspecialties.org) and Dynamic Church Planting International (dcpi.org).

2. John Maxwell, *People Power: Life's Little Lessons on Relationships* (Tulsa: Honor, 1996), 35.

CHAPTER 14

1. An excellent reference for raising personal support is William P. Dillon's *People Raising: A Practical Guide to Raising Support* (Chicago: Moody, 1993).

CHAPTER 15

1. Patrick Lencioni, *The Advantage: Why Organizational Health Trumps Everything Else in Business* (San Francisco: Jossey-Bass, 2012), 168.

CHAPTER 16

1. Organizations providing church-planting training are New Church Specialties (newchurchspecialties.org), Church Multiplication Training Center (cmtcmultiply.org), and Dynamic Church Planting International (dcpi.org).

CHAPTER 17

1. David Garrison, *Church Planting Movements: How God Is Redeeming a Lost World* (Richmond, Va.: International Mission Board, SBC, 1999), 8.

2. Ibid., 9.

3. Ibid., 9–10, emphasis added.

4. Roger Finke and Rodney Stark, *The Churching of America 1776–1990: Winners and Losers in Our Religious Economy* (New Brunswick, N.J.: Rutgers University Press, 1992), 30.

5. Ibid., 52.

6. Ibid., 52–53.

7. Ibid., 56.

8. Ibid., 159.

9. Ed Stetzer and David Garrison, "The Potential for Church Planting Movements in the Western World" (unpublished paper, Exponential Conference, 2008), 5.

10. Ibid.

11. Tom A. Steffen, *Passing the Baton: Church Planting That Empowers* (La Habra, Calif.: Center for Organizational & Ministry Development, 1993), 161.

12. Rodney Harrison, Tom Cheynees, and Don Overstreet, *Spin-Off Churches: How One Church Successfully Plants Another* (Nashville: B&H Academic, 2008), 25.

13. Robert Logan, *Be Fruitful and Multiply: Embracing God's Heart for Church Multiplication* (St. Charles, Ill.: ChurchSmart Resources, 2006), 17.

14. Ibid., 29.

15. Ibid., 30.

16. Ibid., 31.

APPENDIX 1

1. Doris Kearns Goodwin, "Lessons of Presidential Leadership," *Leader to Leader* 9 (Summer 1998): 23–30.

2. Paul Becker and Mark Williams, *The Dynamic Daughter Church Planting Handbook* (San Diego: Dynamic Church Planting International, 1999), 13.

3. Jack Welch, *Winning* (New York: HarperBusiness, 2005), 166.

4. George W. Bullard Jr., *Pursuing the Full Kingdom Potential of Your Congregation* (Atlanta: Chalice, 2005), 11–12.